The Terminal Self

Living at the dawn of a digital twenty-first century, people living in Western societies spend an increasing amount of time interacting *with* a terminal and interacting with others *at* the terminal. Because the self emerges out of inter-action with others (humans and non-humans), this increasingly pervasive and mandatory interaction with terminals prompts a 'terminal self'—a nexus of social and psychological orientations that are adjusted to the terminal logic.

In order to trace the terminal self's profile, the book examines how five unique 'default settings' of the terminal incite particular adjustments in users that transform their perceptions of reality, their experiences of self, and their relations with others. Combining traditional interactionist theory, Goffman's dramaturgy, and the French hypermodern approach, using examples from everyday life and popular culture, the book examines these adjustments, their manifestations, consequences, and resonance with broader trends of a hyper-modern society organized by the 'digital apparatus.'

Suggesting that these adjustments infantilize users, the author proposes strategies to confront three interrelated risks faced by the terminal self and society. These risks pertain to users' subjectivity and need for recognition, to their declining abilities in face-to-face interactions, and to their dwindling abilities to retain control over terminal technologies.

An accessibly written examination of the transformation of the self in the digital age, *The Terminal Self* will appeal to scholars of sociology, social psych-ology, and cultural studies with interests in digital cultures, new technologies, social interaction, and conceptions of identity.

Simon Gottschalk is Professor of Sociology at the University of Nevada, Las Vegas and associate at the International Research Center on Hypermodern Individuals and Society. He served as editor of *Symbolic Interaction* from 2003 to 2007, and as president of the Society for the Study of Symbolic Interaction. Co-author of *The Senses in Self, Culture and Society* (Routledge 2011) and author of *Inter-Face-Work: Symbolic Interaction in the Digital Age*, he has published numerous articles and book chapters that develop a critical interactionist perspective on phenomena as varied as youth cultures, hypermodernism, ethnography, food, environmental identity, mass media, mental disorders, and virtual interactions.

Interactionist Currents

Series editors: Dennis Waskul
Minnesota State University, USA
and
Simon Gottschalk
University of Nevada Las Vegas, USA

Interactionist Currents publishes contemporary interactionist works of exceptional quality to advance the state of symbolic interactionism. Rather than revisiting classical symbolic interactionist or pragmatist theory, however, this series extends the boundaries of interactionism by examining new empirical topics in subject areas that interactionists have not sufficiently examined; systematizing, organizing, and reflecting on the state of interactionist knowledge in subfields both central and novel within interactionist research; connecting interactionism with contemporary intellectual movements; and illustrating the contemporary relevance of interactionism in ways that are interesting, original, and enjoyable to read.

Recognizing an honored and widely appreciated theoretical tradition, reflecting on its limitations, and opening new opportunities for the articulation of related perspectives and research agendas, this series presents work from across the social sciences that makes explicit use of interactionist ideas and concepts, interactionist research, and interactionist theory – both classical and contemporary.

Titles in this series:

The Terminal Self
Everyday Life in Hypermodern Times
Simon Gottschalk

'Doing' Coercion in Male Custodial Settings
An Ethnography of Italian Prison Officers Using Force *Luigi Gariglio*

Microsociological Perspectives for Environmental Sociology
Edited by Bradley H. Brewster and Antony J. Puddephatt

Gendered Bodies and Leisure
The Practice and Performance of American Belly Dance
Rachel Kraus

Challenging Myths of Masculinity
Michael Atkinson and Lee F. Monaghan

The Drama of Social Life
Edited by Charles Edgley

The Politics of Sorrow
Daniel D. Martin

The Terminal Self

Everyday Life in Hypermodern Times

Simon Gottschalk

Routledge
Taylor & Francis Group

LONDON AND NEW YORK

First published 2018
by Routledge

2 Park Square, Milton Park, Abingdon, Oxfordshire OX14 4RN
52 Vanderbilt Avenue, New York, NY 10017

Routledge is an imprint of the Taylor & Francis Group, an informa business

First issued in paperback 2019

British Library Cataloguing in Publication Data
A catalogue record for this book is available from the British Library

Library of Congress Cataloging in Publication Data
Names: Gottschalk, Simon, author.
Title: The terminal self : everyday life in hypermodern times /
Simon Gottschalk.
Description: 1 Edition. | New York : Routledge, 2018. | Series:
Interactionist currents | Includes bibliographical references and index.
Identifiers: LCCN 2017047114 | ISBN 9781472437082 (hbk) |
ISBN 9781315555010 (ebk)Subjects: LCSH: Computers–Social aspects.
Classification: LCC QA76.9.C66 G69 2018 | DDC 303.48/34–dc23
LC record available at https://lccn.loc.gov/2017047114

ISBN: 978-1-4724-3708-2 (hbk)
ISBN: 978-0-367-36954-5 (pbk)

Typeset in Bembo
by Wearset Ltd, Boldon, Tyne and Wear

Contents

Acknowledgments

"So, Simon, what are you doing these days?" Ben, my chiropractor asks, as he is reviewing my chart on his computer screen.
"Writing a book," I answer, a bit hesitantly.
"What about?" he asks; he sounds interested.
"How computers affect us," I answer, pointing at his computer screen.
Ben laughs. "I've got so many stories about that. Would love to read it."

Although typically bearing the name of one or several authors, every book is a collective endeavor and benefits from the help of many individuals. Some of them help in visible and direct ways, others in indirect and invisible ones; sometimes knowingly, sometimes not. First, of course, are our reviewers, editors, and others in the academic and publishing business who encourage us to write, who show patience, and who provide us with the necessary assistance we need to complete that complicated process. This is especially true of Ashgate and Routledge editors, such as Neil Jordan, Shannon Kneis, and Alice Salt. But there are many other and less obvious participants. Our students, colleagues, friends, and relatives who show interest in our work, who share stories with us, ask interesting questions, and point us to interesting directions. Among graduate students, I owe special thanks to Jennifer Whitmer, who helped me with focus group research, with the findings of her own research, and with the lit review. Special thanks also go to Marta Soligo, who located and translated relevant scholarship from Italian and Spanish to English. I am thankful to colleagues and fellow-interactionists such as David Dickens, Robert Futrell, Dmitri Shalin, Joe Kotarba, David Altheide, Kathy Charmaz, John Johnson, Andrea Fontana, Charlie Barnao, and so many others for listening to my ideas, sharing their insights with me, and suggesting interesting avenues for further exploration. This book was also made possible by a sabbatical leave granted by the University of Nevada Las Vegas, and considerably enriched by my collaboration with colleagues at the Paris-based *International Research Center on Hypermodern Individuals and Society*. Among them, I owe special thanks to Nicole Aubert, the Center's founder, who graciously invited me to spend my sabbatical leave there, and who works arduously to steer the hypermodern project. Special thanks also to Canadian scholar Isabelle Fortier for her help with this project.

Last but most important, are our significant others who believe in us, encourage us, and give us the time, space, understanding, and the many other resources we need in order to write. Chief among them is Krystyna, my wife, who never ceases to amaze and inspire me, and who has given me all the support one can only dream of. If not for you …

1   Initializing

Hello.

Please sit down and make yourself comfortable. This is a book. It is not a screen that asks you to scroll, pinch, swipe, or click. There is no 'low battery' warning, no sudden 'temporary unavailability,' no long 'buffering,' no 'error downloading'.' This is a book, and you are in complete control. Hopefully, a physical book such as this one will "make it possible to fend off the nausea roused by the electronic despotism we've let into our lives."[1]

The purpose of this book is to examine how interacting with terminals transforms us as social beings. The *terminal* refers to desktops, laptops, tablets, smart phones, GPS, versatellers, iwatches, surveillance cameras, Google glasses, and all those network and internet-enabled devices that take us online and enable us to interact with others. According to a recent report, there are currently 4.9 billion connected terminal devices in the world, and this number is projected to increase about fourfold by 2020.[2] While I could have selected the words 'virtual,' 'cyber,' or 'digital' to describe the contemporary self, these terms refer exclusively to *online* experiences. However, it is becoming increasingly difficult to distinguish offline from online domains. As Baym and boyd remark, "offline contexts permeate online activities, and online activities bleed endlessly back to reshape what happens offline."[3] Psychologist Aboujaoude puts it more boldly: "Saying we have successfully logged off is an expression of seriously wishful thinking. Most of us are never truly offline anymore."[4] Accordingly, our interactions with terminals impact, and are impacted by, our offline moods, thoughts, intentions, interactions, relationships—in short, what makes us human. And as we increasingly find ourselves at the terminal, the terminal increasingly finds itself inside us, whether we're looking at it or not, whether we consciously realize it or not. As the site par excellence where offline and online merge, the terminal evokes well the idea of a portal between those two once-distinct domains of experience. So, my first reason for selecting the concept terminal is because it evokes this merging of offline and online experiences in ways that words such as virtual, cyber, or digital do not.

My second reason for selecting the concept terminal is because, as an adjective, it refers to a stage in the life of organisms, objects, and processes.[5] This connotation allows for (hopefully interesting) double-entendres that adjectives such as virtual, cyber, or digital do not. However, those double-entendres are not always intended to be playful. As a growing number of scholars soberly analyzing contemporary trends (especially those destroying the natural environment) from a variety of disciplines warn, we cannot realistically continue along the trajectories we are currently racing along. If we do, we will bring about the terminal phase in the life of the planet and of humanity. For Bauman also,

> The gradual, yet merciless disintegration of the structures on which our shared civilization has rested threatens consequences of which the politicians do not speak, of which the public is unaware, and which most of our contemporaries are unable to grasp and visualize, let alone predict. Never before has the sociologist's intervention been as urgent and imperative as it has become of late.[6]
>
> (Rojek 2004, 311)

Hence, the adjective 'terminal' articulates this more serious meaning as well.

The *terminal self* refers to social psychosocial orientations that characterize individuals living in contemporary Western societies—an admittedly large and diverse collection of people.[7] The idea that different periods in the history of a society prompt particular psychosocial dispositions in its citizens has a rich tradition in modern social sciences. For example, in the early decade of the twentieth century, Georg Simmel described the 'metropolitan type,' and in the 1930s, Karen Horney diagnosed *The Neurotic Personality of Our Time*. In the 1950s Theodor Adorno and his colleagues exposed *The Authoritarian Personality*, and that same decade saw the rise of William Whyte's *Organization Man*, Herbert Marcuse's *One Dimensional Man*, and David Riesman's 'other-directed personality.' In the 1960s, Jay Lifton unveiled the *Protean Self*, and in the 1970s, Christopher Lasch analyzed *The Minimal Self*. In the 1980s, scholars such as Wood and Zurcher recognized a 'postmodern self,' and Sherry Turkle found a *Second Self* emerging online. In the 1990s, Kenneth Gergen announced the *Saturated Self*, and in the early 2000s, Zhao and Karge outlined the profile of the *Digital Self*. There are many more, of course, but you get the point. C. Wright Mills suggested that assessing the psychosocial dispositions that come to dominate (in) a particular historical moment is a key insight of the sociological imagination and a critical type of information that helps us understand this moment better, navigate it more intelligently, and, when necessary, transform it.

The theoretical orientations we select inevitably shape what and how we think, what we find worthy of study, what kind of data we collect, how we do so, and what we do with it. This book is not different. Informed by both critical theory and symbolic interaction theory, the *terminal self* is not just another intellectual exercise, a line on my CV, or an intellectual pose. My attempt to understand the dispositions fostered by the omnipresent terminal is also political: I want to challenge them, raise awareness about the risks they present, and suggest ways to resist them. My belief that we should resist these terminal effects is inspired by Frankfurt School sociologist Hartmut Rosa, who reminds us that real human suffering—whether recognized as such or not—should be the normative starting point of critical theory. For him, the most promising path to develop this theory is to critically examine existing social practices and arrangements in light of how social actors define the 'good life': "Social conditions that undermine our capacity for auto-determination and that erode our potential for individual and collective autonomy can and must be identified and criticized because they systematically prevent people from realizing their conceptions of the good life."[8] The conditions that facilitate or inhibit the "good life" pertain to the distribution of not only material resources, but of psychological ones as well. And since the distribution of such resources increasingly also occurs (and in unique ways) at the terminal, I am interested in understanding how the dispositions it promotes help or hinder our quest for "the good life."

Having grown up BG (Before Google), I acknowledge, salute, and am endlessly amazed by the phenomenal power of the terminal devices we access every day, and for so much of the day. Rainie and Wellman remind us that "it has become a cliché that we carry in our smartphones more computing power than the first manned space flights did."[9] The idea that lightly swiping across the screen of a thin and sexy pocketsize box activates so many functions was—when I was young—pure science fiction. This disorienting power should give us pause to consider whether there is not some truth to the claim that the invention of the internet (and our mobile access to it) is as critical to human evolution as the invention of fire. Or to Castells' suggestion that it is "the most extraordinary technological revolution in humankind."[10] However, as incredible as it is and as powerful as it makes us feel, interacting with terminals is also prompting new experiences of social reality, ways of thinking, of experiencing the self, of perceiving others, and of treating them. And not always in desirable directions. Accordingly, this book is openly partisan. I fully acknowledge the positive potentialities that the terminal enables, but also believe that they pale in comparison to their troublesome effects.

Educating myself about the terminal, I found the hypermodern perspective most pertinent to the topic at hand and most elaborate in light of its critical angle and its multidisciplinarity. A secondary goal of this books is therefore to introduce this perspective to American audiences. However, rather than launching into abstract discussions of the finer theoretical points of the hypermodern perspective, I *apply* it in my assessment of the terminal self. Hopefully, this "doing rather than showing" will be a more effective way of communicating (about) this perspective.

Show hidden files

Before proceeding, two caveats are in order. The first concerns conceptual boundaries. As we are increasingly surrounded by terminals, spend more time interacting with them, and interact with them to complete an increasing number of functions, it is difficult to pronounce statements about the terminal that would hold true for all of our online activities. While there will always be exceptions, I focus especially on e-mail, smartphones, texts, social media postings, surveillance technologies, and internet browsing. Those are the most frequent types of terminal use. Terminal devices can perform many functions even when they are not connected to the internet, but we purchase them mainly to go online.[11] Most users access the terminal to connect with others and to find information, and both objectives require going online. Commercial ads incite us to purchase a terminal device or to upgrade the one we own by praising its esthetic qualities and the lifestyles it symbolizes, but they especially emphasize the promise of increased online speed, power, reach, and performance.

The second caveat is that writing a book about a terminal self will immediately prompt charges of technological determinism, so allow me to address those before we start. Going at least as far back as Socrates, the introduction of new technologies in a society has predictably provoked alarmed pessimism, fervent utopianism, and every nuance in between. Considering this fascinating history of technology, it would be perfectly reasonable to advance that the terminal is just another tool, that there is nothing new under the sun, and nothing to worry about.[12] However, deciding whether this concern about the terminal is warranted or whether it merely repeats an old and tired tune cannot be satisfactorily answered either way. In the end, the conclusion one reaches is a messy—albeit informed—synthesis of theoretical leanings, partial and incomplete knowledge derived from constantly updated research, agreement with insights proposed by experts in the field, personal experience, and biography. In this book, I develop the position that the terminal is a unique type of technology. Challenging many assumptions we often make about the relations between humans and their tools, it invites us to ask new questions and think differently.

Marshall McLuhan suggested that we shape our technologies and that they shape us. Whether it's a microscope or Microsoft, technologies have 'preferred encodings'; they are designed to be used in prescribed ways, and have—to quote Bauman—"manipulated probabilities."[13] To operate them efficiently, users must perform certain skeletal, muscular, sensory, cognitive, or neural movements rather than others. Those then become habitual, taken-for-granted, and incorporated in their routine physical activities, perceptual and sensory apparatus, mental processes, and consciousness.

Those effects are especially intensified when the technologies in question are mental ones.[14] Technologies materialize, articulate, and promote social perceptions of reality. They are "genuine social indicators of what a society thinks of itself, how it represents itself, and hence realizes itself," suggests French sociologist Dubey.[15] For Nicholas Carr, intellectual technologies such as terminals embody "an intellectual ethic, a set of assumptions about how the human mind works or should work." More importantly, they also transmit this ethic "into the minds and culture of its users."[16] For Levy,

Technology has become a major component of my ideology and of most people's, at least in the sense of "ideology" that refers not to a set of opinions but to actual behaviors and rituals that integrate people into social structures. Insofar as electronic devices determine our actual behavior on a day-to-day basis, it is not too much to say that ideology is engineered.[17]

As pioneer in digital media design Jaron Lanier explains, ideological preferences are literally encoded into the softwares that operate the terminals of everyday life:

when developers of digital technologies design a program that requires you to interact with a computer as if it were a person, they ask you to accept in some corner of your brain that you might also be a conceived of as a program ... Different media designs stimulate different potentials in human nature.[18]

In so doing, "machines can and do accelerate trends, magnify cultural weaknesses, and fortify certain social structures while eroding others," writes Douglas.[19] For Baym, technologies "do not make history by themselves. But some kinds of machines help make different kinds of histories and different kinds of people than others."[20] Terminals are no different. They colonize the landscape and tweak the mindscape. And they do so faster and deeper than any other technology. As Rushkoff puts it, they are:

the windows through which we are experiencing, organizing, and interpreting the world in which we live ... They are the interfaces through which we express who we are and what we believe to everyone else ... They are fast becoming the boundaries of our perceptual and conceptual apparatus; the edge between our nervous systems and everyone else's, our understanding of the world and the world itself.[21]

Of course, we do not have to submit to the terminal's 'preferred encodings.' We can disable, enhance, resist, or subvert them. But such decisions often take time, energy, reflection, specialized knowledge, equipment, and skills—especially when the technologies in question are as complex as terminal devices. Most people do not—and, one fears, cannot—choose the path of technological resistance against the terminal. They have a difficult enough time just remaining reasonably competent interacting with it, responding promptly and appropriately to its swelling flood of information, all the while adjusting to the constantly changing upgrades, versions, add-ons, virus threats, warnings, options, privacy policies, etc.[22]

As the mobile node of an increasingly expanding digital apparatus, the terminal is not just a tool or device like, say, Hemingway's *Underwood* typewriter. It is part of a technological *meta-system*. It articulates a 'digital logic,' "a systemic force that transcends the power of any single technology."[23] And in contrast to other technologies, terminal devices evolve. They become smarter, smaller, and faster. They share information and make decisions. They can scan your eyes and sense your movements. They can track you down, let you in, or lock you out. They are—to quote Dator et al.—'mutative technologies' that are "once again redefining what it means to be humans living on a planet mutating faster than ever ..."[24] In both theoretical and applied endeavors, therefore, it seems a bit irresponsible—and often quite hazardous—to handle technologies as neutral tools, and to insist that only human interpretations and use matter. Of course they matter, but that is only one variable in an increasingly complex—and perhaps obsolete—equation. As Harris suggests, "Every technology will alienate you from some part of your life. That is its job. *Your* job is to notice. First notice the difference. And then, every time, choose."[25]

List folders

To develop this book, I have combined theoretical scholarship about the internet and hypermodernism with interdisciplinary research on individuals' interactions with terminals. I integrate this academic scholarship with what I have learned from my own research and professional activities. More precisely: I've conducted focus groups with undergraduate students where they discussed interpersonal conflicts prompted by e-mail communication, and have reviewed their essays discussing internet use and dependence. I've analyzed graduate students' essays about their terminal interactions, and have collaborated with them on virtual ethnographies in *Second Life*. Outside of academic walls and away from students, I have intervened in actual cases of cyber-incivility in the workplace and the private sphere, and have delivered workshops on computer-mediated communication to a variety of medical, commercial, and educational organizations, both in the US and Europe. In Fall 2014, I had the good fortune of spending a sabbatical semester in Paris, at the International Research Center on Hypermodern Individuals and Society, where I collaborated with other scholars to develop the hypermodern project and the present book.[26]

I have organized this book in eight chapters. In "Settings," I discuss the distinctive French hypermodern perspective to analyze contemporary society. Since the current historical moment or setting is so intertwined with the rise of computer technology, I introduce here the idea of a 'digital apparatus'—a nascent social system that is organized, powered, and expanded by computer technology. The terminal is just a mobile node of this apparatus, and according to some, so are we. When discussing computers, the concept 'settings' also refers to the controls of a hardware or software that are preset by their manufacturers. Using that metaphor, I also briefly introduce here five unique *terminal* 'default settings,' imperatives, or features that literally structure our interactions with terminals and induce distinctive psychosocial dispositions. In the next five chapters I examine those five default settings one by one, trace the psychosocial dispositions they promote in the terminal self, and discuss their manifestations in the hypermodern everyday.

One first terminal default setting is *interactivity*. In order to participate in everyday life, we constantly have to interact with terminals. To do so, we must align our thinking to its logic. In "Sync," I discuss four types of cognitive adjustments we must implement when interacting with terminals, propose the concept of 'software thinking,' and examine the consequences of this mental style for the terminal self's cognitive aptitudes and perceptual habits.

These enforced adjustments to the terminal logic are facilitated by *customization*—our ability to adjust our terminal to our individual preferences—at least on the surface. However, in order to adjust the terminal to our self-image, we must also adjust our self-image to the terminal. In "Personalize," I discuss this second default setting, distinguish between three levels of personalization, and examine the sorts of adjustments they induce in users' perceptions of their places in the hypermodern present.

As an increasingly important setting for self-presentation, self-reflection, and self-evaluation, the terminal requires constant *visibility*, a third default setting or imperative. Yet, the kind visibility the terminal self is constantly summoned to perform is deformed by technological exigencies. Guided by Axel Honneth's theory of social recognition, I examine in "Validate" how users adjust to this third terminal default setting, and how those adjustments shape their need for recognition in the hypermodern present.

A fourth terminal default setting is *connectivity*—the constant imperative to communicate with others, to interact with them. In "Ignore," I combine Goffman's insights on face-work with Honneth's theory of social recognition to examine the unique challenges users encounter when interacting with others at the terminal, to discuss how they manage these difficulties, and to assess how those adjustments guide their interpersonal relations, both at the terminal and away from it.

The terminals that permeate our lives are equipped for *surveillance*, the fifth default setting. Our activities at (and away from) the terminal produce enormous quantities of data that reveal a great deal about what we do, where we're going, how we respond to information, what we like, what we share, etc. This data is combined into an increasingly detailed digital 'profile' that is used to evaluate us, to calibrate the types of resources we can access, to predict our future behaviors, and to manipulate them. Moreover, new generations of terminals are increasingly equipped for programed autonomy and—some experts fear—will soon be capable of complete autonomy. In "Submit," I discuss the assault on the right to privacy by the new conditions of near-total surveillance, examine how users adjust to these conditions, and consider the dangers these adjustments pose to individual's sense of integrity and privacy. I conclude this chapter by reviewing the even more serious dangers posed by the rapidly evolving powers of mutating terminal technologies.

These five default settings and their associated psychosocial dispositions pertain to five different levels of experience. Thus, *Interactivity* pertains to the *cognitive and perceptual* level. *Personalization* refers to subjective experience and the sense of *individuality*. *Visibility* pertains to the intrapersonal level—the *sense of self* and the need for *recognition*. *Connectivity* is concerned with the interpersonal level of *social interactions*. Finally, *Surveillance* refers to the institutional level, and to one's sense of *privacy* and *integrity*. Of course these five default settings are neither exhaustive nor mutually exclusive, and one could organize them very differently. I have used them as tools to organize and present the material included here. Thus, I do not want to draw too sharp dividing lines between these five default settings, the psychosocial dispositions they incite, and the levels at which they operate (see Table 1.1).

In "Disable," I suggest that, in concert, the dispositions prompted by terminal interactions *infantilize* users; they disempower and disable them. Reviewing scholarship on infantilization in various social institutions both in the US and in other societies, I suggest that this condition should be added to acceleration, excess, and visibility as a defining aspect of hypermodern culture.

Table 1.1 Chapter titles, terminal default settings, psychosocial adjustments, level

Chapter titles	Terminal default settings	Psychosocial adjustments	Level
Chapter 1 "Sync"	Interactivity	Decreased agency, autonomy De-skilling Urgency De-realization Software thinking	Sensory Motor Cognitive/perceptual
Chapter 2 "Personalize"	Customization	Self-centeredness Instant gratification Immediacy	Subjectivity
Chapter 3 "Validate"	Visibility	Anxiety Self-inflation Omnipotence Hyper-other-directedness Extimacy	Intrapersonal Sense of self
Chapter 4 "Ignore"	Connectivity	Declining role-taking Detachment Dehumanization Loss of empathy	Interpersonal Sense of the other
Chapter 5 "Submit"	Surveillance	Loss of freedom Powerlessness Distrust Loss of privacy, integrity Submissiveness	Institutional Sense of generalized other

In the concluding "Save as" chapter, I distill the ideas presented in the book as three major risks that the terminal self must successfully resolve. Focusing on the intrapersonal, the interpersonal, and the institutional levels, I suggest a variety of strategies that will hopefully assist in and inspire such resistance.

Click next to continue.

Notes

1 Giraldi (2015).
2 Barker (2014).
3 Baym and boyd (2012), 327.
4 Aboujaoude (2011), 278.
5 i.e., final, last, ending, lethal, fatal, etc.
6 Rojek (2004), 311.
7 I use the term "psychosocial dispositions" as a shortcut to refer to: routine ways of (a) experiencing the self, the social world, and one's place in it, and (b) perceiving others and interacting with them.
8 Rosa (2012), 69–70.
9 Rainie and Wellman (2012), 277.
10 Castells (2006), 5.
11 According to recent journalistic reports, every terminal device is now connected to the internet, whether we choose to or not, whether the terminal is on or off. According to other reports, our terminals can now also be activated remotely and unbeknownst to us.
12 Baym (2010).
13 Bauman and Lyon (2013), 79.
14 Gillespie (2003), 9.
15 Dubey (2001), 275.
16 Carr (2011), 45.
17 Levy (2011).
18 Lanier (2010), 4–5.
19 Baym (2010).
20 Ibid.
21 Rushkoff (2011), 138–139.
22 Olmstead and Smith (2017).
23 Hassan (2009), 133.
24 Dator, Sweeney, and Yee (2015), 109.
25 Harris (2014), 206.
26 *Centre International de Recherches sur l'Individu et la Société Hypermodernes.*

References

Aboujaoude, Elias. 2011. *Virtually You: The Dangerous Powers of the E-Personality*. New York: W. W. Norton & Co.

Barker, Collin. 2014. "25 Billion Devices by 2020 to Build the Internet of Things." ZDNet November 1. Available at: www.zdnet.com/article/25-billion-connected-devices-by-2020-to-build-the-internet-of-things. Retrieved November 13, 2014.

Bauman, Zygmunt and David Lyon. 2013. *Liquid Surveillance*. Cambridge, UK: Polity.

Baym, Nancy K. 2010. *Personal Connection in the Digital Age*. Cambridge, UK: Polity.

Baym, Nancy K. and danah boyd. 2012. "Socially Mediated Publicness: An Introduction." *Journal of Broadcasting & Electronic Media* 56(3): 320–329.

Carr, Nicholas. 2011. *The Shallows: What the Internet is Doing to Our Brains*. New York: W. W. Norton & Co.

Castells, Manuel. 2006. "The Network Society: From Knowledge to Policy." pp. 3–21 in *The Network Society: From Knowledge to Policy*, Manuel Castell and Gustavo Cardoso (eds.). Washington, D.C.: Center for Transnational Relations.

Dator, James A., John A. Sweeney, and Aubrey M. Yee. 2015. *Mutative Media: Communication Technologies and Power Relations in the Past, Present, and Futures*. Lecture Notes in Social Networks. Switzerland: Springer International Publishing.

Dubey, Gérard. 2001. "Les Systèmes d'Information et de Communication ou Comment les Sociétés Se Pensent." pp. 273–285 in *Nouvelles Technologies et Modes de Vie: Aliénation ou Hypermodernité?*, Philippe Moati (ed.). Paris: Éditions de l'Aube.

Gillespie, Tarleton. 2003. "The Stories Digital Tools Tell." pp. 1–21 in *New Media: Theses on Convergence Media and Digital Reproduction*, John Caldwell and Anna Everett (eds.). New York and London: Routledge.

Giraldi, William. 2015. "Object Lesson: Why We Need Physical Books." *New Republic*, Retrieved April 19. www.newrepublic.com/article/121560/bibliophiles-defense-physical-books.

Harris, Michael. 2014. *The End of Absence: Reclaiming What We've Lost in a World of Constant Connection*. New York: Current.

Hassan, Robert. 2009. *Empires of Speed: Time and the Acceleration of Politics in Society*. Leiden: Brill.

Lanier, Jaron. 2010. *You are Not a Gadget: A Manifesto*. New York: Vintage

Levy, Matthew. 2011. "A Notion of Faces, Not Laws: Facebook as Ideological Platform." *Fast Capitalism* 8(1): Retrieved June 11, 2015. www.uta.edu/huma/agger/fastcapitalism/8_1/levy8_1.html.

Olmstead, Kenneth and Aaron Smith. 2017. "What the Public Knows About Cybersecurity." Pew Research Center on Internet and American Life, March 22. Retrieved June 9, 2017. www.pewinternet.org/2017/03/22/what-the-public-knows-about-cybersecurity/.

Rainie, Lee and Barry Wellman. 2012. *Networked: The New Social Operating System*. Cambridge, MA: MIT Press.

Rojek, Chris. 2004. "The Consumerist Syndrome in Contemporary Society: An Interview with Zygmunt Bauman." *Journal of Consumer Culture* 4(3): 291–312.

Rosa, Hartmut. 2012. *Aliénation et Accélération: Vers une Théorie Critique de la Modernité Tardive*. Paris: La Découverte.

Rushkoff, Douglas. 2011. *Program or be Programmed: Ten Commands for a Digital Age*. Berkeley, CA: Soft Skull Press.

Simmel, Georg. 1965. "The Metropolis and Mental Life." pp. 409–424 *in The Sociology of Georg Simmel*, K. H. Wolff (ed.). New York: Free Press.

2 Settings

> Who is too blind to see that a profound mutation is being advocated here? A new dismembering and a complete reconstitution of the human being so that he can at last become the objective (and also the total object) of techniques.[1]

The concept 'setting' refers first to a contemporary moment that, as the opening quote suggests, is propelled by accelerating transformations on many levels of society. In their attempts to understand this setting and to outline its unique characteristics, scholars have used terms such as 'liquid,' 'late modern,' 'radical modern,' 'ultramodern,' 'supermodern,' 'postmodern,' and 'hypermodern,' among others. Of all those terms, the 'postmodern' is perhaps the most recognized one in the arts, popular culture, and especially academia, where it has generated quite a bit of intellectual activity. While some scholars use postmodern and hypermodern interchangeably, others insist that we should distinguish between these two terms, as they evoke different phenomena and approaches.[2]

The idea of a French hypermodern perspective is a bit problematic. It a dynamic and interdisciplinary *mélange* of scholarship hailing from Germany, Great Britain, the US, Spain, Canada, Brazil, and other countries, but it still suggests a distinctive French flavor. Its general headquarter is the CIRISHYP (International Research Center for the Study of Hypermodern Individuals and Society), housed at the École Supérieure de Commerce de Paris.[3] As its mission statement indicates, the CIRISHYP studies:

- The impact of new information and communication technologies on individuals' behaviors and lifestyles.
- The consequences of the society of hyperconsumption and the integration of the commercial mindset in individuals' everyday life.
- The types of expression and individual consequences of a *new relation to time* ... *new relations to others* ...; and *new relations to the self.*
- New working styles that are linked to new technologies, and their consequences on individual and collective life.

The research conducted by the Institute is pluridisciplinary (sociology, marketing, psychology, economics, management, history, philosophy).[4] Inspired by critical humanism, focusing on the psychosocial level, relying on rigorous—and especially—micro-level research, attentive to cultural phenomena, and integrating broad macro-social trends in its analysis, the hypermodern approach highlights acceleration and excess as defining qualities of the contemporary moment.

Considering those broad brushstrokes, you might wonder what the hypermodern perspective shares with symbolic interactionism. While few hypermodernists mention Mead, Cooley, Blumer, or Goffman,[5] they echo the symbolic interactionist tradition in a number of ways. For example, they emphasize the centrality of interaction, the self, meaning, and emotion for making sense of the self-in-society.[6] As I develop in the "Validate" and "Ignore" chapters, the hypermodern project is also inspired by Frankfurt School sociologist Axel Honneth's concept of social recognition, a concept that articulates fundamental symbolic interactionist principles. The methods hypermodernists use also resonate with the symbolic interactionist tradition, as they include naturalist observations, in-depth interviews, qualitative case-studies, focus groups, and the critical interpretation of mass media texts. While some might object to audible Freudian accents, Phillip Manning has documented how Freud's influence was woven into the fabric of the early Chicago School.[7] Hypermodern scholars are also openly critical and integrate the broader societal landscape in their analysis as they seek to understand how historically-specific social arrangements bear upon individuals, their everyday interactions, struggles, experiences, and psychosocial orientations. In other words, how they prevent individuals from achieving 'the good life.' Here too, the affinities with the symbolic interaction tradition are numerous. For example, Shalin's work reminds us that George Herbert Mead was clearly inspired by humanitarian socialism and a progressive agenda.[8] Michael Schwalbe has discussed the contributions of a Meadian ethics for Marxist sociology[9] and many scholars inspired by C. Wright Mills provide inspiring examples of blending a critical agenda with the symbolic interactionist project.

Clear history and select all

In contrast to postmodernists who announce the *end* of modernity, hypermodernists are concerned by its radical *acceleration*. For Frankfurt School sociologist Hartmut Rosa, the various waves of acceleration unleashed by the industrial revolution are central to understand the history of modern society and the present.[10] Assessing the manifestations of this increasing acceleration in the technological, institutional, and subjective realms, he calls our attention to its decidedly oppressive nature. Following this approach, hypermodern scholars have focused especially on the acceleration of four key processes that launched and propelled modernity—the market, the individual, democracy, and science. For urban sociologist François Ascher, this acceleration of modern trends is especially visible in:

> individuation, or individuals' desire for an expanding autonomy and a particular appropriation of the world; an increasing social differentiation and interaction that positions individuals in increasingly complex networks and systems; a growing reflexivity that feeds the ambition to master the world, that replaces traditions by routines, and that mobilizes scientific knowledge to reach its objectives. It is also visible in a marketization that forcefully drags increasingly numerous social practices into the economic field, and in increasingly numerous and subtle collective regulations that organize social life in very complex societies.[11]

For Rosa, acceleration violently disintegrates social institutions, rushes everyday experience, and shatters subjectivity. He thus suggests a revision of Marx's various forms of alienation through the prism of acceleration, and adds *alienation from time and space* as other important dimensions of this famous concept. As Rosa explains, at the subjective level, acceleration leads to disintegration and detachment. Disintegration, because we fail to integrate the various episodes of everyday experience (and the commodities we acquire there) into a holistic and long life-project. As a result of this disintegration, we become detached and disengaged from the times and spaces of our lives, from our experiences, and from the material objects with which we live and work. Unsurprisingly, "this disposition obtains in the realm of social relations as well."[12]

Let us flesh out those ideas in the sphere of work, for example. Today, a growing number of professions in the hypermodern economy enable, and often require, employees to work—often at a terminal—from a variety of locations, across different time zones, and on the go. Thus, while the Agro-Industrial economy was located in the work*place* (the factory plant, the field, the ocean, the mine), the hypermodern one is located in work*time*. Now, the question is no longer, *where* we work, but *for whom* and *how*. This temporal and spatial dislocation of work is significant on many levels. Marx suggested that, as a space, the factory plant provided industrial workers with the concrete structure where they could literally see their common plight, recognize their common interest, develop class consciousness, and mobilize to implement social change. If the workplace is a space that could inspire solidarity with physically co-present workers, worktime encourages soli*tary*ty—the freedom to personalize one's labor according to one's lifestyle, preferences, and predilections, often in isolation from co-workers. While it is evidently convenient for many and has countless advantages, this dislocation of workplace to worktime is transforming both the life-project of work and the interpenetration between work and personal life. If workers can increasingly leave the office, now the office never leaves them. Thus, while an increasing number of white-collar and knowledge workers are given more freedom to manage the time and space of their labor, they are also simultaneously expected to work more—often at a mobile terminal—and often during their newly gained 'free' time. As a familiar example, an increasing number of workers are now unofficially expected to attend to work-related e-mails, messages, and phone calls after hours, on week-ends, and on holidays. As Juréguiberry reports in his research on French workers' use of cell phones:

> Emergency is no longer limited to the professional sphere but is increasingly invading the private one. One of the main causes of this phenomenon is the professional exploitation of telecommunicational ubiquity. Physical distance walls, work schedules no longer protect: every day, increasingly, professional emergencies erupts in the professional space, colonizing it ...[13]

As Rosa reminds us, however, in order to accomplish more in a given amount of time, we must necessarily accelerate the tempo of our activities, take less time between them, or perform more of them in the same unit of time. As I am typing these words, my terminal prompts me to attend to the e-mails piling up in my mailbox, to back up my work, to install an upgrade, to remember an appointment, and to consult a dictionary. When the number of tasks we must accomplish increases in the same unit of time, we switch to an 'urgent' mode. And when such a mode becomes *de rigueur*, it can have detrimental effects on those subjected to it. To wit, in their research in various French commercial enterprises, Nicole Aubert and Vincent De Gaulejac document the disastrous psychosocial "costs of excellence" exacted by the neo-liberal workplace. As they find, its new regime of urgency produces alarming rates of burnout, harassment, and other symptoms of emotional and psychosomatic disorders that decimate otherwise diligent and motivated employees.[14] As Jauréguiberry also finds, many respond to this sense of urgency by developing a 'connectivity syndrome.' Its symptoms include:

> the anxiety of wasted time, the stress of the last minute, the constantly frustrated desire to be here and elsewhere at the same time, the fear of missing out on something important, the dissatisfaction of hasty decisions, the fear of not being connected at the right time on the right network, and the confusion resulting from an ephemeral information saturation.[15]

It goes without saying that accelerating our performance in work-related activities necessarily also transforms how we perform our leisure activities, how we manage our everyday life, interact with others, etc. Hence, it is not just the acceleration of work-related activities that is concerning, but also the tempo at which hypermodern individuals must live, as many of the social institutions in which they participate find themselves accelerating at an irrational and dysfunctional pace. As Bauman notes, in contemporary society "progress is no longer thought about in the context of an urge to rush ahead, but in connection with a desperate effort to stay in the race."[16] For Claudine Haroche, increasing social acceleration "might progressively so overwhelm individuals that they can no longer understand what they are doing and the world in which they live ... Lacking distance, time, or intelligibility, they must submit to a permanent change that requires endless adaptability."[17]

Rosa also points out that while the contemporary moment is propelled by an uncontrollable acceleration in the domains of technology, social institutions, and everyday experience, it is also disrupted by the clashing of various temporal modes. Some areas of society (technology, for example) show vertiginous rates of acceleration while others (public administration, for example) seem static in comparison. In everyday life too, we experience these temporal misalignments in those common instances when the various social environments through which we circulate are 'out of sync' with each other and collide. It is a little bit like rushing through traffic to reach the airport on time, only to find oneself delayed at the security check-in line. At the terminal, those experiences are frequent as well. It is like grabbing your phone, bursting with excitement because you want to communicate an intense emotion right now, only to discover that there is 'no available network.' Or being hit with the realization that the text that took you hours to produce has suddenly and permanently disappeared. Or sending an urgent e-mail to someone who remains inexplicably silent.

Assessing the destabilizing impact this acceleration wreaks on social institutions, theorists wonder whether we should not also accelerate our theoretical models so as to better understand the present, or on the contrary, whether we should slow them down.[18] In any case, maintains Rosa,

> a critical analysis of the temporal structures of society, of its accelerators, and of the alienation it creates is the only rationally valid option in a world that has become too fast and unstable to allow an in-depth analysis of its characteristics.[19]

Acceleration might have become routine, but it is neither benign nor innocent. For Rosa, it is a new totalitarian power that is both *internal to* and *of* modernity. Like other forms of totalitarian power, acceleration meets the four following criteria:

> a) it exerts pressure on the wills and actions of subjects ... b) it is inescapable, i.e. all subjects are affected by it ... c) it is all-pervasive, i.e. its influence is not limited to one or the other area of social life, but to all aspects of it ... and d) it is hard or almost impossible to criticize and fight it.[20]

In addition, and perhaps in contrast to other forms of totalitarian power, the logic of acceleration is profoundly irrational. In any case, it "must be criticized in the same way as every other form of totalitarian domination."[21]

Hypermodern theorists also suggest that *excess* is a distinctive characteristic of the present. For Nicole Aubert, "the essential mode of hypermodernity is excess, the overabundance of the event."[22] She sees hypermodern society as one where:

> everything—consumption, competition, profit, the search for pleasure, violence, terrorism, capitalism—is exaggerated, pushed to the limit and to an outrageous level. It results from the globalization of the economy, the generalized flexibility that it produces, the ever-increasing levels of performance, adaptability and reactivity that it requires, and the profound modification in our behaviors that it induces ... It is also a society captured by the triumphant mercantile logic and shaken by the explosion of all the limits that had until now structured the construction of individual identities. It is a society where everything is apparently possible but that also mercilessly rejects those who cannot follow the pace of its requirements.[23]

For Cournut, the hypermodern era is characterized by a disorienting "collusion between the temptation toward excess and the means to achieve it."[24] Meeting neither resistance nor alternatives, this logic of excess and intensification is noticeable in the arts, in religious fundamentalism, in the spheres of production, of administration, and of the management of cultural activities.[25] As I have also discussed in another paper, this logic is especially audible in the language of everyday life, in commercial ads, and in public pronouncements by politicians and media figures.[26] Characterized by the abuse of superlatives, the language of excess both normalizes and reinforces those institutional trends.

In contrast to (some) postmodernists who sought to understand the effects of rupture and the end of grand narratives in cultural phenomena, many hypermodernists confront the effects of acceleration and excess in cultural, interpersonal, and subjective ones.[27] The combined—and synergetic—impact of these forces in so many realms of the contemporary everyday cannot help but profoundly disorient and shock hypermodern citizens, who, by necessity, respond to it in a variety of ways. For Nicole Aubert, our accelerated relation to time takes the form of instantaneity and urgency. While individuals might experience instantaneity as a sense of omnipotence, mastery, and freedom, others experience urgency as a form of coercion, of tyranny, and violence, as they are forced to always accomplish more in less time.[28] Suffering from a chronic state of distraction,[29] stressed by the pressures of instantaneity, and rushed by a compressed temporality, 'instant individuals' are unable to learn from a rapidly disappearing past, and are incapable of projecting themselves in the future.[30] 'Individuals by excess,' they quickly crash and burn out in the flames of constant hyperactivity. On the other end of the continuum are the 'individuals by default'—the disaffiliated who are denied consideration, security, stable relations, anchors, or support. Accordingly, the two poles of contemporary individualism are the anxieties of excess and the anxieties of emptiness. The former is a response to "excesses of affectivity, of violent stimulations, of love, of hatred, of rage, of despair, and of exaltation." The latter is a response to "sentiments of psychic emptiness characterized by the painful inability to feel, to think, and to imagine." For Claudine Haroche also, the hypermodern moment is:

> simultaneously despairing and hyper-hedonist. It is a society where uncontrollable technologies that intrude the mental sphere seem to modify perceptual and sensory functioning at a profound level. These contribute to the formation of a culture of sensations and visual impressions. They partially annihilate critical thought, and simultaneously promote ... narcissism and egocentrism.[31]

As a result, the hypermodern self is characterized by "superfrivolity, a shrinking of interior space, the loss of a sense of existence, a lack of sensitivity to others, a blocked ability to reflect, political and moral disengagement, and a reduction of morality."[32]

For these reasons perhaps, hypermodern theorists have paid special attention to the new form of depression that seems to prevail in the contemporary moment. As Nicole Aubert explains, if traditional forms of depression were characterized by moral pain or sadness, its contemporary symptoms are deceleration and inertia: "Forced to act at all costs and always faster ... contemporary individuals experience less the constraint of renunciation (permitted/prohibited) than that of limits (possible/impossible) ... If neurosis is a drama of culpability, depression is the tragedy of inadequacy."[33]

This new form of depression is also perhaps a response to a pervasive fear that intensifies the experience of acceleration and excess. Far from being irrational, this fear is fanned by a number of obvious macro-social trends. Canadian sociologist Sébastien Charles provides a partial list:

> a globalist logic indifferent to individuals, an exacerbated liberalism of competition, the deepening of inequalities, a hectic engineering of information technologies, and a volatilization of labour with stagnant and worryingly high levels of unemployment in the wake of spiraling financial crises that seem as though never to end. The reign of hedonism surely continues unabated, entertainment options explode, but these fail to offset that rising anxiety that is so characteristic of hypermodernism.[34]

Accordingly, if disenchantment, fragmentation, and cynicism were the hallmark emotions of postmodernism, the hypermodern moment presents us with quite different dispositions that are both promoted and enhanced by our terminal interactions.

The digital apparatus, the mode of interaction, and the terminal self

Manuel Castell announces the 'network society,' which he defines as "the social structure resulting from the interaction between the new technological paradigm and social organization at large."[35] In his analysis, the digital networks of communication are as much the 'backbone' of the network society as the power networks were the infrastructure of the industrial one. For hypermodern theorist Ascher also, information has become the new source of raw material that plays the same role in the hypermodern economy as steel did for the industrial one.[36]

Where Marx indicted an industrialist regime that brutalized workers' bodies, the digital apparatus rewires users' brains—their thoughts, perceptions, emotions, dispositions, and even neural activity.[37] Where the industrial apparatus is oppressive, loud, material, and relatively predictable, the digital one is user-friendly, silent, symbolic, and rapidly mutating. Where the conspicuous factory is the concrete space of the industrial apparatus, the terminal is the mobile and miniaturized node of the digital one. Where power rests in the hands of those who own of the means of production in an industrial order, it rests in the hands of those who own the means of interaction and surveillance in the digital apparatus. Where a monolithic industrial order homogenized workers, consumers, and commodities, the digital apparatus offers users near-perfect personalization and customized validation. It does not coerce as much as it seduces; one algorithm per person, and at a highly affordable price. In such conditions, terminal selves do not live an alienated existence only because they have lost control over the conditions under which they must labor, but also because they have lost control over the codes with which they must interact and participate in society.[38] Since, to quote Hassan, "computerization is the technological means of speed"[39] the terminal is the increasingly mobile node of this digital apparatus, where we learn, adopt, and transmit a new mode of interaction. And since interaction is the engine of society, the basic social act, the source of a consensual reality and of selfhood, the terminal self that emerges through such interactions presents important mutations, that merit investigation. As I try to develop in this book, this investigation pertains to much more than individuals and their terminals. For Gopnik (2005),

> the digital world is new, and the real gains and losses of the Internet era are to be found not in altered neurons or empathy tests but in the small changes in mood, life, manners, the feelings it creates—in the texture of the age.[40]

Default settings

Scholars attempt to understand the effects of this new mode of interaction by conducting large-scale surveys that assess significant changes in indicators of computer use and social psychological health in the population. They also use naturalistic observations of users interacting with terminals, and with each other when terminals are present. They analyze texts that can reveal such information, conduct participant observation and experiments in virtual spaces, and engage users in in-depth interviews. As a growing volume of scholarship attests, these methods are quite useful to understand the transformations unleashed by the new mode of interaction. While I frequently refer to this scholarship, I especially focus here on the terminal itself, and especially its settings, as those prompt particular kinds of subjective experience, of perception, and of interaction.

In conversations about computers, the concept 'settings' refers to the controls of a hardware or software that are preset by their manufacturers. Understanding those settings and the softwares that activate them is important. For Manovich,

> What electricity and the combustion engine were to the early 20th century, software is to the early 21st century ... If we want to understand today's techniques of communication, representation, simulation, analysis, decision making, memory, vision, writing, and interaction, we must understand software.[41]

Accordingly, he explains, when an increasing volume of interactions, skills, cultural experiences and decisions are taking place at terminals that are controlled by large software systems, we should start asking—among others—"How does the software we use influence what we can express and imagine?"

Social scientists typically concur that how we use and think about a technology is informed by our experience with it, and such experience is invariably shaped by biography and history. For example, like many members of my generation and social class, I grew up operating technologies such as: transistor radios, Walkmans, bulky television sets one had to operate manually, vinyl record-players, acoustic and electric musical instruments, analog tape recorders, celluloid-based cameras, landline telephones, massive video-game consoles, mechanical typewriters, and various mechanical tools that are typically used for home-maintenance, car-repair, sewing, cooking, and farming. Today, like a majority of individuals living in this society and many others, I use many terminal devices on any regular day, albeit reluctantly. This reluctance is generational and has its advantages. As Michael Harris notes, individuals who grew up before the rise of the terminal and who now have to adapt to its logic have the advantage of being able to compare this logic to a very different earlier one. Such comparisons then help us better recognize what we have gained thanks to the terminal, but especially what we are losing because of it.[42] Although prehistoric by today's standards, the devices I grew up with are not only practically useful—they help us get the job done—but also abstractly so, as they help us to critically examine our relations to technology. In other words, those devices are also useful tools to think with.[43]

The terminal comes equipped with five interrelated "default settings" that are significantly different from pre-terminal technologies: *Interactivity, Customization, Visibility, Connectivity,* and *Surveillance.* In the next five chapters, I review these default settings one by one, assess the psychosocial dispositions they induce in the terminal self, and examine their parallels with hypermodern trends.

Notes

1 Ellul (1964), 348.
2 See Redhead (2011).
3 Centre International de Recherches sur l'Individu et la Société Hypermodernes.
4 www.escpeurope.eu/faculty-research/research-centres-and-research-laboratories-escp-europe-business-school/cirishyp-centre-international-de-recherches-sur-lindividu-et-la-societe-hypermodernes-escp-europe/. I have translated from French to English all the citations by hypermodern scholars that appear throughout this book.
5 Francis Jauréguiberry (2003) directly engages George Herbert Mead and uses foundational Symbolic Interactionist concepts. See also Caludine Haroche (2011).
6 As became clear in informal conversations with European sociologists, no other contribution by American Sociology prompted as much recognition and enthusiasm as the Chicago School. Adam Gopnik's recent article about Howard Becker's popularity in Paris confirms this personal Impression.
7 Manning (2005).
8 Shalin (1988).
9 Schwalbe (1989).
10 Rosa (2012, 2010); Rosa and Sheuerman (2009).
11 Ascher (2007), 60.
12 Rosa (2012), 132.
13 Jauréguiberry (2003), p. 2.
14 See also Aubert (2003).
15 Jauréguiberry (2005), 91.
16 Bauman (2007), 103.
17 Haroche (2011), 80.
18 Gane (2006).
19 Rosa (2012), 139.
20 Rosa (2013), 61.
21 Rosa (2012), 85; see also Gottschalk (1999).
22 Aubert (2005), 14–15.
23 Aubert (2006a).
24 Cournut (2005), 64.
25 Tapia (2012), 19.
26 Gottschalk (2009).
27 As I develop in Chapter 4, the condition of visibility is also increasingly being recognized as an important aspect of the hypermodern moment.
28 Aubert (2008a), 25; see also Aubert (2008b and 2006a).
29 Jackson (2009).
30 Aubert (2008a), 31.
31 Tapia (2012), 19.
32 Ibid.
33 Aubert (2003), 173.
34 Charles (2009), 395.

35 Castells (2006), 60.
36 Ascher (2000), 81.
37 See Bauerlin (2011); Carr (2011); Turkle (2011); Vannini, Waskul, and Gottschalk (2011).
38 The two are of course related.
39 Hassan (2009), 120.
40 Gopnik (2015).
41 Manovich (2013).
42 Harris (2014).
43 See especially Turkle's *Simulation and Its Discontent* 2009.

References

Ascher, François. 2000. *La Société Hypermoderne*. Paris: Éditions de l'Aube.
Ascher, François. 2007. *Examen Clinique: Journal d'Un Hypermoderne*. Paris: Éditions de l'Aube.
Aubert, Nicole. 2003. *Le Culte de l'Urgence: La Société Malade du Temps*. Paris: Flammarion.
Aubert, Nicole. 2005a. "Un Individu Paradoxal." pp. 13–24 in *L'Individu Hypermoderne*, Nicole Aubert (ed.). Toulouse: Érès.
Aubert, Nicole. 2006a. "Sur L'hypermodernité et de la Société Hypermoderne." *Next Modernity* 10:30.
Aubert, Nicole. 2006b. "Hyperformance et Combustion de Soi." *Études* 405(10): 339–351.
Aubert, Nicole. 2008a. "Violence du Temps et Pathologies Hypermodernes." *Cliniques Méditerranéennes* 78: 23–38.
Aubert, Nicole. 2008b. "Les Pathologies Hypermodernes: Expressions d'Une Nouvelle Normalité?" *Revue Internationale de Sociologie* 18(3): 419–426.
Bauerlin, Mark (ed.) 2011. *The Digital Divide: Arguments for and Against Facebook, Google, Texting, and the Age of Social Networking*. New York: Jeremy P. Tarcher.
Bauman, Zygmunt. 2007. *Liquid Life*. Cambridge, UK: Polity.
Carr, Nicholas. 2011. *The Shallows: What the Internet is Doing to Our Brains*. New York: W. W. Norton & Co.
Castells, Manuel. 2006. "The Network Society: From Knowledge to Policy." pp. 3–21 in *The Network Society: From Knowledge to Policy*, Manuel Castell and Gustavo Cardoso (eds.). Washington, D.C.: Center for Transnational Relations.
Charles, Sébastien. 2009. "For a Humanism Amid Hypermodernity: From a Society of Knowledge to a Critical Knowledge of Society." *Axiomathes* 19. 389–400.
Cournut, Jean. 2005. "Les Défoncés." pp. 61–71 in *L'Individu Hypermoderne*, Nicole Aubert (ed.). Toulouse: Érès.
Ellul, Jacques. 1964. *The Technological Society*. New York: Alfred A. Knopf.
Gane, Nicholas. 2006. "Speed Up or Slow Down? Social Theory in the Information Age." *Information, Communication & Society* 9(1): 20–38.
Gane, Nicholas. 2011. "How the Internet Gets Inside Us." *The New Yorker*. Retrieved February 14, 2014. www.newyorker.com/magazine/2011/02/14/the-information.
Gopnik, Adam. 2015. "The Outside Game: How the Sociologist Howard Becker Studies the Conventions of the Unconventional." *The New Yorker*. January 12. www.newyorker.com/magazine/2015/01/12/outside-game. Retrieved January 13, 2015.

Gottschalk, Simon. 1999. "Speed Culture: Fast Strategies in TV Commercials." *Qualitative Sociology* 22(4): 311–329.

Gottschalk, Simon. 2009. "Hypermodern Consumption and Megalomania: Superlatives in Commercials." *Journal of Consumer Culture* 9(3): 307–327.

Haroche, Claudine. 2011. "L'invisibilité Interdite." pp. 77–102 in *Les Tyrannies de la Visibilité: Être Visible Pour Exister?*, Nicole Aubert and Claudine Haroche (eds.). Toulouse: Érès.

Harris, Michael. 2014. *The End of Absence: Reclaiming What We've Lose in a World of Constant Connection*. New York: Current.

Hassan, Robert. 2009. *Empires of Speed: Time and the Acceleration of Politics in Society.* Leiden: Brill.

Jackson, Maggie. 2009. *Distracted: The Erosion of Attention and the Coming Dark Age.* New York: Prometheus.

Jauréguiberry, Francis. 2003b "Internet Comme Espace Inédit de Construction de Soi." pp. 223–244 in *L'Internet, Nouvel Espace Citoyen?*, Francis Jauréguiberry and Serge Proulx (eds.). Paris: l'Harmattan.

Jauréguiberry, Francis. 2004. "Hypermobilité et Télécommunication." pp. 130–138 in *Les Sens du Mouvement: Modernité et Mobilités dans les Sociétés Urbaines Contemporaines*, S. Allemand, F. Ascher, and J. Lévy (eds.). Paris: Belin.

Jauréguiberry, Francis. 2005. "L'Immédiaté Télécommunicationnelle." pp. 85–98 in *Nouvelles Technologies et Modes de Vie: Aliénation ou Hypermodernité?*, Philippe Moati (ed.). Paris: Éditions de l'Aube.

Manning, Phillip. 2005. *Freud and American Sociology.* Cambridge, UK: Polity.

Manovich, Lev. 2013. "The Algorithms of Our Lives." *Chronicle of Higher Education.* Retrieved December 19, 2013 http://chronicle.com/article/The-Algorithms-of-Our-Lives-/143557/?cid=at&utm_source=at&utm_medium=en.

Redhead, Steve. 2011. *We Have Never Been Postmodern: Theory at the Speed of Light.* Edinburgh University Press.

Rosa, Hartmut. 2010. *Accélération: Une Critique Sociale du Temps.* Paris: La Découverte.

Rosa, Hartmut. 2012. *Aliénation et Accélération: Vers une Théorie Critique de la Modernité Tardive.* Paris: La Découverte.

Rosa, Hartmut. 2013. *Alienation and Acceleration: Towards a Critical Theory of Later Temporality.* Malmögade, Denmark: NSU Press.

Rosa, Hartmut and W. E. Sheuerman (eds.) 2009. *High-Speed Society: Social Acceleration, Power, and Modernity.* Philadelphia, PA: Pennsylvania University Press.

Schwalbe, Michael L. 1989. "Meadian Ethics for Marxist Psychology." *Berkeley Journal of Sociology* 34: 87–104.

Shalin, Dmitri. 1988. "G. H. Mead, Socialism, and the Progressive Agenda." *American Journal of Sociology* 92: 913–951.

Tapia, Claude. 2012. "Modernité, Postmodernité, Hypermodernité." *Connexions* 1: 15–25.

Turkle, Sherry. 2009. *Simulation and Its Discontents.* Cambridge, MA: MIT Press.

Vannini, Phillip, Dennis Waskul, and Simon Gottschalk. 2011. *The Senses in Self, Society, and Culture: A Sociology of the Senses.* New York: Routledge.

3   Sync

One first unique default setting of the terminal is that it is *interactive*. In order to operate it, we must *interact with it*. And we must do so very differently than with, say, a telephone, a typewriter, or a toaster. Activating the terminal requires a different engagement than acting on it mechanically, like dialing up a number on a rotary telephone, pressing on a key to raise a lever, or pushing a knob down. To activate the terminal's functions, we must orient ourselves to it, adjust our thinking to it, and incorporate its logic. We must 'sync' to it, and in order to do so, we must adopt particular assumptions, modes of attention, rules, practices, and gestures. In addition, and in contrast to a telephone, a typewriter, a toaster, a speed bump, a door-stopper, and other familiar objects that theorists often use as exemplars to discuss the agency of technologies,[1] the terminal also *interacts with us*. It reacts to our behaviors, asks us questions, requires that we take particular decisions and perform particular gestures, to which it responds in an emerging and potentially endless dialogue. It literally remembers what we do and adjusts itself for future interactions. In contrast to those other technologies, the terminal's type of interactivity is intelligent and evolving. It is scripted by programs that enable it to change. The terminal is also a narrative object in the most literal sense of the term.[2] It collects data about every user and can, on demand, produce a narrative about them. While this narrative is mostly limited to a display of information about a user's activities, interactions with others, places, and times, it is increasingly oriented toward predictions, and will soon be capable of producing its own narratives, and without humans' intervention. In other words, the terminal might soon reverse the often-used model whereby a technician (human being) uses technique (creativity, skills, knowledge, scripts) to operate a technic (a tool) with which s/he transforms the environment. In this case, the technic (the terminal) uses and produces technique (creativity, skills, knowledge, scripts) to interact with and transform technicians (human beings).

While many technologies induce physical changes in users by requiring distinctive body motions, the terminal induces cognitive and perceptual changes in its users by imposing on them a unique form of interactivity. As tools of the mind, they "amplify and in turn numb the most intimate, the most human, of our natural capacities—those for reason, perception, memory, emotion."[3] In this chapter, I focus on five features of terminal interactivity: *necessity and ubiquity*, *simplification*, *urgency*, *de-realization*, and what I call *software thinking*. Note also that the five main features of terminal interactivity I discuss below are neither exhaustive nor mutually exclusive and some of these features might also be present in other technologies than the terminal. However, no technology but the terminal includes all of them. In other words, trying to understand how terminal interactivity affects users cannot be limited to just a listing of its properties (unique or not), but in their synergetic effects in particular historical conditions.

Log-in required: necessity and ubiquity

One first feature of terminal interactivity is that it is necessary and ubiquitous. It is useful to remember that pre-terminal technologies such as television sets, telephones, radios, freezers, electric appliances, cameras, etc. were not mandatory for participation in everyday life. Individuals could function quite effectively for long periods of time without using them, or lived without them altogether. As children, we knew people who owned very few of those devices and seldom assumed that they suffered from social exclusion, boredom, boorishness, or deprivation as a result. The technologies that populated everyday life seemed neither necessary nor ubiquitous, and one could encounter a wide spectrum of technological usages.

Today, in order to participate competently in society, we *must* interact with terminals. From locating a journal article to looking for a job, from purchasing music to booking a trip, from selecting a doctor to reserving a hotel room, there is no escape and no relief. As Hassan puts it, we are increasingly becoming victims of 'digital slavery'[4] and are growing dependent on the terminals of the networked society because "we *need* to be connected to live and work and to be part of the 'normal' mainstream of networked life."[5] Thus, rather than seeing terminal technologies as just additional tools people *choose* to use in order to connect with others or locate information,[6] we no longer have a choice but *must* interact with them. As we increasingly interact with multiplying terminals to meet a growing catalog of needs, and as once dispersed sources of cultural information all migrate to the terminal, it becomes near-impossible to imagine society, interactions, and everyday life that are free of terminal interventions.

As a simple exercise, try to monitor how many terminals you interact with on any regular working day, how many times a day, what you do with them, and how long you spend on each one of them. Also reconstitute all the steps that would be necessary to accomplish the same function without interacting with a terminal, and the time it would take to do so. Conversely, try to spend any regular working day without once interacting with any terminal, and record what happens. And, to add a little edge to the experiment, try to record as honestly and accurately as possible how you react when the terminal is unavailable in those very moments when you want to use it. Indeed, Bodford and her research team find that "almost a third of a sample of American adults have reported that their mobile devices are 'something they can't imagine living without,' with almost half deeming their attachment to these devices 'an addiction'."[7] In the end, however, it matters little whether one owns a terminal or not, or whether one uses it a lot or just a little.[8] It has already become part of our everyday life and it is already re-coding it. For urbanist Adam Greenfield,

> the most basic tasks we undertake in life now involve the participation of a fundamentally different set of actors than they did even ten years ago. Beyond the gargantuan enterprises that manufacture our devices, and the startups that develop most of the apps we use, we've invited technical standards bodies, national-and supranational-level regulators, and shadowy hackers into the innermost precincts of our lives. As a result, our ability to perform the everyday competently is now contingent on the widest range of obscure factors—things we'd simply never needed to worry about before, from the properties of the electromagnetic spectrum and our moment-to-moment ability to connect to the network to the stability of the software we're using and the current state of corporate alignments.[9]

Just click: simplification

A second feature of terminal interactivity is the simplified type of engagement it invites. Pre-terminal technologies perform distinctive functions and operate according to specific principles. Recording a conversation, for example, demand a different engagement, knowledge, gestures, and skills than taking pictures, calling someone on the phone, typing a note, playing the *Space Invaders* video-game, consulting one's calendar, or locating oneself on a map. These functions are also encased in separate devices, and many of those have their designated places in our home. The old clock is on the mantle, the maps are in the living room bookcase, the landline telephone is on the small table in the hallway, and the big calendar is on the kitchen wall, left of the fridge. Today, we can perform all these very different activities and an infinity more on the go, at the same terminal devices, many of which fit in our pockets, on our wrists, or under our arms. As Greenfield put it:

> In short order, the smartphone supplanted the boombox, the Walkman and the transistor radio: all the portable means we used to access news and entertainment, and maybe claim a little bubble of space for ourselves in doing so. Except as ornamentation and status display, the conventional watch, too, is well on its way to extinction, as are clocks, calendars and datebooks. Tickets, farecards, boarding passes, and all the other tokens of access are similarly on the way out, as are the keys, badges and other physical means we use to gain entry to restricted spaces.[10]

There is little doubt that one can experience a great deal of pleasure from "making things happen" on the terminal screen. And while recent technological inventions such as TouchScreen enhance this pleasure as well as provide new experiences of visual–digital integration[11] in the end, the haptic sensations the terminal provides are reduced to light vibrations, pressing on plastic keys, rolling plastic trackballs, pulling on plastic triggers, rotating plastic joysticks, scrolling little plastic wheels, and performing simple finger gestures on plastic screens. In other words, these tactile sensations are monotonous, limited, and repetitive. While the virtual objects I can manipulate with my mouse and keys might be represented as endowed with a wide variety of textures, temperatures, resistances, velocities, weights, sizes, etc., the physical sensations they produce remain pretty much the same.

The reduction of tactile sensations to the repetitive manipulation of—and contact with—plastic objects is consequential for the development of cognitive and physical skills as well. As Franks reminds us:

> Mead … gave highest priority to touch as the primary sense organ in his theory of the act. We now know that the sense of touch and the hand takes the largest amount of sensory cortex in the human brain by far. Mead as well as Damasio conceived perception as a readiness to act, and subliminal muscular movements accompanied perception in preparation for the act.[12]

As such, embodied action, especially "that activity involved in tactile, contact, manipulative behavior is also the ground of language and thought," writes Franks. As he explains: "The new field of cognitive semantics makes the important claim that much of our knowledge is grounded in, and structured by, patterns of our bodily actions and the indifferent requrements of the manipulative objects."[13]

This simplification not only stunts the exercise of concrete motor skills and more abstract cognitive ones, however; it is also consequential for emotional well-being. As Montagu reminds us, touch is "like a human need, since it confers security and belonging …".[14] Accordingly, the reduction of this quintessential sense to its terminal applications may also explain the increasing problems of attachment noted in hypermodern individuals.[15]

Google Earth

The GPS is another example of this terminal-induced degradation of the quasi-universal skill of geo-location—or a person's ability orient oneself in the environment and to navigate intelligently in it. Like the fate of so many other essential skills degraded by terminal interactivity, geo-location shrinks from being a mode of embodied attention that mobilizes memory, the senses, 'gut feelings,' etc. to become an effortless, passive, and decontextualized following of 'directions.' As Carr puts it: "the automation of wayfaring distances us from the environment that shaped us. It encourages us to observe and manipulate symbols on screens rather than attend to things in real places."[16]

As media critic John Ebert sees it, Google Earth is more than an app; it is a metaphysics.[17] Characteristically, he notes, there are no recognizable people on this virtual planet. Sometimes, they appear as faceless and blurry silhouettes, but they are inconsequential to one's progress because, on Google Earth, the user's point of view is the only one that matters. As the omnipresent and omnipotent observer, I can look at any location from outer space as easily and effortlessly as from the street level.[18] Looking at the GPS terminal that simulates my changing position, the very landscape through which I advance is continuously morphing to re-adjust itself around me and to continuously position me at its center. At the simple graphic and interactive level, the GPS terminal advances a particularly disorienting understanding of the relation between self-and-environment.

This technological affordance may not sound so terrible, and it goes without saying that a GPS can be quite useful. However, as anthropologist Ingold suggests, "wayfaring is our most fundamental way of being in the world,"[19] and one suspects that this technologically-induced ineptitude is not limited to physical environments but is replicated in societal ones as well. As I develop in the next three chapters, the terminal self finds it increasingly difficult to commit to long-term objectives, is unsure about how to get there, uncertain about the sorts of future these objectives hold, and constantly distracted along the way. As the objectives are frequently re-defined in mid-course, as the paths to reach them are constantly re-routed, and as the speed of travel is invariably fast or faster, the GPS seems indeed the perfect app for the terminal self, whose very survival in the hypermodern economy depends on rapid mobility. However, there is a price to pay for this cognitive shortcut. As a research on London taxi drivers documents, for example, those who rely on a GPS to navigate around the city show structural changes in their brains.[20] Such structural changes obtain among other categories of users than taxi drivers, and co-occur with transformations induced by the other features of terminal interactivity.

Slide and swipe, click and skip, pinch and scroll. As the number and variety of functions we can/must now activate at the terminal grow exponentially, the expert manual skills one acquired by the increasingly dexterous and intelligent manipulation of concrete objects become artless gestures on the high-def plastic screens of eerily similar terminals that remain mysteriously opaque, frequently unresponsive, and inexplicably self-destructive. As terminal interactivity is becoming increasingly ubiquitous and necessary, the sort of tactile engagement it rewards necessarily also deteriorates language and thought.

In some sense, the artless manual gestures we must perform to interact with terminals already articulate—and invite—the distinctive type of mental engagement we exercise there. The more we rely on this simplified form of interactivity and are rewarded when we do so well, the less likely we are to sustain pre-terminal ways of knowing and skills. In turn, the less developed those skills and ways of knowing are, the less confident we feel in their applications, and the more likely we are to turn to terminal interactivity and shortcuts, in a rapidly escalating vicious cycle. As a result, we disregard different ways of knowing, limit the range of our experiences, our imagination, and our intelligence, and forget the skills that were once needed to perform all the functions that we now casually delegate to the terminal. As Seremetakis reminds us, "memory ... is a culturally mediated practice that is activated by embodied acts and semantically dense objects."[21] Our reduced ability to remember, let alone deploy alternatives then weakens our ability to resist the digital apparatus' hegemony.

Click now: urgency

In "Settings," I discussed the importance hypermodern scholars assign to acceleration as a main force of the present moment, a force that transforms the technological, the institutional, and the subjective realms. In contrast to Wajcman who notes that "there is no temporal logic inherent in an artefact that determines time practices"[22] I suggest that terminal interactivity does precisely that by normalizing and intensifying this sense of urgency. This third feature of terminal interactivity operates at three interrelated levels.

We experience this sense of urgency at a first and implicit level simply by interacting with the terminal. When we turn it on, activate it, or click, the terminal immediately responds and prompts us to respond. Concretely, it asks us to select and enter information, and as soon as we do, it typically reacts instantly. Such a rapid response time naturally invites us to follow suit, to 'sync' to the tempo of terminal interactivity, and to accelerate our own response time. As terminals become faster and more responsive, this unusual rapidity of response becomes normalized, and we may come to expect that all our intentions should be attended to with the now expected immediacy of "instant download." Importantly therefore, terminal interactivity rewards quick responses to 'urgent' commands rather than promoting the kind of long and deep reflection necessary to calmly assess the long-term consequences of one's actions. This is especially worrisome in light of the sense of de-realization and ephemerality prompted by terminal interactivity, a point I develop below.

"Last Call!" "Red Alert!" "Urgent Reminder!" "Critical!" "Instant Poll!" "Last Chance!" "Breaking News!" "Terrible News!" "Important Request!" "Serious Announcement!" "Response Overdue!" "Reminder: Give Us Your Feedback!" "Open Immediately!" "⚠ Sign Immediately!" On a second, and interpersonal level, we experience a sense of urgency because of the implicit and explicit pressures to respond quickly to terminal messages. While the storm of 'urgent' warnings listed above would perhaps be 'normal' if my networks were composed of emergency personnel, they regularly appear in e-mails sent by political organizations, commercial enterprises, and academic institutions, among others. Thus, Derks et al. find that "inherent in e-mail communication is the expectation that people can be reached easily and quickly."[23] As Turkle also notes, this expectation is even more compelling when individuals communicate via text messages.[24] Discussing those, Baym finds that "autonomy is increasingly constrained by the expectation that we can be reached for communication anytime, anywhere, and we will owe an appropriate and timely response."[25] In France, Jauréguiberry observes that this obligation to constantly be on call so intensifies dependency relations as to make them too heavy to bear. As he puts it,

> the too numerous urgent e-mails or texts sent by a supervisor or a colleague, the too frequent calls from a spouse or a worried mother, the too numerous notifications from our social networking sites produce a deterioration, an erosion and a tiredness that is manifested in bursts of exasperation, of mood swings, in a sentiment of saturation, and of overflowing.[26]

As the number of messages multiply, and as many require a prompt answer, we find ourselves having to accelerate the process by which we attend to, classify, and respond to these competing demands for attention. To complicate matters, those demands are articulated in different registers (personal, professional, serious, funny, gloomy), and invite different types of responses and subjectivity. Family members, trusted friends, colleagues, supervisors, assistants, political parties, charity organizations, community groups, and even bots seek our attention by summoning different aspects of our self. Continuously, indiscriminately, and sometimes simultaneously. As Rushkoff puts it,

> we reduce the length and complexity of our responses ... making almost everything we transmit sound like orders barked over a walkie-talkie in a war zone ... But those commands are coming at us now in increasingly rapid bursts, stimulating us to respond at rates incompatible with human thought and emotion—and in ways that are not terribly enjoyable.[27]

"Only 1 room remaining at this rate," the little red icon flashes repeatedly on the *Bookings.com* website. "Only 6 seats remaining at this price," warns the message on the *Spirit Airlines* one. On a third level, the sense of urgency we experience at the terminal is also prompted by very explicit commands that we act quickly if we want to secure resources or avoid undesirable outcomes. Trying to reserve hotel rooms, plane seats, train tickets, concert tickets, and many other commodities or services, the multiple webpages that intrusively pop up all warn me—each in its own way—that I need to decide quickly and 'click now' in order to secure whatever resource is now available *only* at the terminal. Hidden in small print are the dire warnings of penalties I will incur if I commit an error, if I click on the wrong selection, or if I miss a key piece of information floating somewhere in a constantly 'updated' visual logorrhea of multi-sized, multi-fonts, multi-colored words, numbers, and pictures. As I am sure many readers can attest, trying to repair such mistakes can be frustratingly time-consuming, complicated, and punitive. While other technologies have also transformed Western individuals' relation to time, they did so by re-*organizing* our relation to it, by *structuring* it differently.[28] In contrast, terminal interactivity completely disintegrates our relation to time by shrinking it to a constant and urgent present that restricts our sense of autonomy and agency.

Double-click: de-realization

In *Simulation and Its Discontent*, Turkle remarks that the technological shift to simulation and immersion "can tempt its users into a lack a fealty to the real."[29] Terminal interactivity cultivates this tendency by inducing *de-realization*. The traditional definition of this condition suggests: "experiencing self, others, and the external world generally as if through an invisible wall or screen." In contrast, the sort of de-realization prompted by terminal interactivity presents new symptoms that, one suspects, partly result from the sense of *ephemerality* users experience there. They do so in at least seven different ways.

Upgrade now

"A New iPhone Every Year," promises the *Apple* ad. The terminal is of course a physical object, but in contrast to pre-terminal devices that were often preserved during one's lifetime and transmitted across generations, we are discouraged from keeping our terminal devices for very long. To reduce any nascent sense of attachment, multiplying commercial ads are constantly urging users to 'upgrade'—to get newer, faster, more powerful, more fun, and more versatile models. And since every new generation of terminals performs better and faster than the previous one, resisting this prompt to upgrade results in restricted access to resources, less performativity, slower response time, malfunctioning, inability to use particular applications, etc. In other words, those seemingly 'fun' upgrades are in fact coercive. And as companies release with much fanfare the new model to crowds of giddy shoppers, they are already working on the next generations. This ephemerality of the terminal as physical object resonates with the switch from "physical" to "moral" consumption,[30] and the fleeting nature of attachment in the hypermodern present. For Bauman,

> consumer goods are not meant to be durable; their fast ageing, rapid loss of allure and seductive power is perhaps their main attraction. They promise not to outstay their welcome, not to clutter the space of which we always 'need more,' not to survive their power to bring satisfaction … They would rather advertise their 'biodegradibility' or similar wondrous

inclination to commit suicide once no more needed. They are meant for instant use, an instant satisfaction that does not require a lengthy training—a gratification without delay; they are also meant to accept their falling out of favour once their time is over and agree in advance to leave quietly with no reproof, acrimony and grudge.[31]

Adam Greenfield also notes the "dematerialization of everyday life"[32] and recent psychological research suggests that hypermodern individuals replicate such dispositions toward the people with whom they form social relations.[33] As Aubert notes, they trade durable and binding commitments for brief, superficial, fragile, and interchangeable encounters that end as quickly as they start.[34] Psychologist Serge Tisseron also find hypermodern individuals to be "motivated by denial, disengagement, and a fear of abandonment that they soothe by short-term associations, temporary, tentative, and opportunistic commitments that are emotionally intense, replaceable, and disposable."[35] And as the psychological motivations behind such short-term associations necessarily shape their trajectories and temper, it might also be worth understanding how they disintegrate and with what effects.

If planned obsolescence is not new, its overt celebration as economic principle and psychological orientation is. Forced to constantly trade our terminals for newer and better performing models, we do not just sign in on our new devices, we also—every four years or so—confirm a new way of relating to objects, and beyond that, to people, and to reality itself. As Rosa notes, such ways of relating generate neither attachment nor appropriation nor identification.[36]

File not found

We also experience ephemerality as a result of repeatedly having to adjust to the terminal's changing functioning and content. I have in mind here the successive waves of operating softwares, apps, websites designs, icons, themes, lay-outs, add-ons, that populate the terminal and enable its operations. As an example that I am sure you can recognize, my smartphone is very different today than what it was six months ago. To be honest, I don't really remember what it looked like six months ago. It is—materially—the same device, and some icons, pictures, apps, and programs have remained. But others have been—*autonomously*—added, replicated, removed, upgraded, or filed in different areas of the memory. In contrast to other technologies, the functioning of our terminal devices is constantly changing, in *spite* of our preferences, and even without our intervention. Thus, while most technologies typically require pre-determined and fixed types of adjustment (whether physical or mental), terminal interactivity imposes a regime of *constant* and *changing* adjustments. As Rosa suggests,

> While material objects are becoming increasingly complex, I become increasingly stupid about them; in fact, I lose some of my cultural and

practical knowledge. This results directly from the devaluation of experience on behalf of innovation. Similarly, I become alienated in my relation to material objects that I own, in the sense that I feel bad because I do not treat them well. I feel rather guilty towards them. They are so valuable and are so intelligent, and I use them like an idiot.[37]

We also experience ephemerality when we must adjust to random disappearance and loss of content. Inexplicably, files disappear, programs are purged, e-mails vanish, playlists are wiped out, documents are corrupted, messages are lost, songs cannot be played, photo albums are unaccountably emptied, datasets do not 'transfer,' and hard drives crash. A password I have used for years suddenly becomes "invalid," and clicking on a bookmarked link now leads to a defunct website.[38] As Rosa reminds us, the importance of the stability of objects with which we live and work is not limited to those objects, as those "are to some degree constitutive of our identity."[39] Hence, these experiences of ephemerality in terminal content spreads to interpersonal relations as well. At the terminal, people can inexplicably interrupt or discontinue written exchanges, and others suddenly disappear from our networks, as we disappear from theirs. To state the obvious, pre-terminal technologies were fairly static. They could be decorated or moved to a different place in our home, but—unless they were stolen, damaged, or destroyed—they would not randomly disappear or shift content. They provided a certain sense of stability that physically grounded users' relationships to objects in general, and to other aspects of their environment as well.

Download app

While we might invest quite a bit of money and time to personalize, protect, extend, and accessorize our terminals, and while we can use terminals without necessary connecting to the internet, we mainly use them to access a constantly growing array of *digital* resources. Those resources are intangible; they are but codelines, algorithms.[40] I have in mind here the internet and phone "plans" we must purchase, the music and books we can download, the reach of our wireless service, the softwares that will unlock the miracles and wonders of computing technology, the virtual storage capacity we can own, the graphic and sonic quality of our experiences, the reliability and security of our network systems, the level of privacy which will shield us, and the quality of technical support we can expect when—panicked—we find our terminals paralyzed, contaminated, and hacked.[41]

This increasing desirability and consumption of non-material resources is also a most interesting aspect of the hypermodern economy. As as recent research in consumer trends reveals, youth prioritize easy *access* to goods and services rather than ownership.[42] Granted, gargantuan amounts of material goods continue to be invented, produced, marketed, and consumed in hypermodern societies. Granted also that—from extraction to disposal—the manufacturing of terminal devices and other material goods requires the suicidal destruction of natural resources and the criminal exploitation of human labor. As critical researcher Christian Fuchs reminds us,

> The existence of the Internet in its current dominant capitalist form is based on various forms of labor: the relatively highly paid wage work of software engineers, low-paid proletarianized labour in Internet companies, the unpaid labour of users, highly-exploited bloody Taylorist work, highly-toxic e-waste labour that disassembles ICTs, and slave work in developing countries, producing hardware and extracting "conflict minerals."[43]

And granted also that the enduring feeding frenzy for material goods is producing volatile islands and mountains of waste, some of which are clearly toxic.[44]

Still, without minimizing the psychological motivations underlying hypermodern consumption, its 'moral' rather than 'physical' dimension, and the eroticized features of hypermodern commodities,[45] we should also add *intangibility* as a key aspect of the (digital) resources hypermodern consumers purchase at the terminal in order to manage their everyday lives efficiently, quickly, and comfortably. To complicate matters, the terminal is also increasingly becoming a main conduit to (quasi-instant) access to *material* resources, through online shopping for example. A TV commercial ad can make us fantasize about a certain product; terminal interactivity can bring it to our doorstep.[46]

Authorize computer

The ephemeral quality of those resources hypermodern individuals access at the terminal replicates in their sense of *ownership* of these resources. Is the software boasting "100 Millions Hits" I just downloaded mine? Can I share it? Duplicate it? Transfer it to another terminal? Can I share a scholarly article I just downloaded for free with 20 graduate students? If I download a picture from the terminal and alter it, can I then upload it and claim it as mine?

We might own the terminal in our hand, but not necessarily the resources we access with it. Music is a good example. Up until a couple of decades or so ago, you knew you held a vinyl music record in your hands. It was a concrete and often enchantingly esthetic object you had borrowed from a friend, received as a gift, bought at the store, or stolen. Unless you had borrowed it, it clearly belonged to you. You could write your name on the album jacket, listen to it on any player in the world, record it on tape, offer it, symbolically break it, frame it, or glue it in an artsy avant-garde collage. There was an it. At the terminal, however, a music record becomes a virtual folder, and the digitally encoded songs become individual 'downloads,' each with its own price tag.[47] Stranger yet, I can now play 'my' music on a maximum of five 'authorized' and compatible computers. In this way also, terminal interactivity enhances our experience of ephemerality by completely destabilizing our experience of appropriation and ownership of the objects we daily use and work with.

Cut/copy/paste

This experience of ephemerality and de-realization spreads to the integrity of the digital resources themselves. To continue with the music example, when the Beatles released the canonical *Sergeant Pepper's Lonely Hearts Club Band* in 1967, musicians, records-producers, critics, and fans understood that a rock album could be much more than just a collection of songs. It could be an integrated text that tells a story, sustains an unmistakable theme, evokes a particular mood, and unfolds in a clear sequence you had to follow in order to really 'get it.'[48] At the terminal, however, we can extract any digital song from its original musical context, download it, and pair it with any other downloaded song in infinite numbers of changing permutations. In addition, we can now also manipulate the digitized song itself. We can remove some of its sections, re-order their sequence, increase their speed, insert loops, sound effects, silences, etc.[49] Our sense of ephemerality at the terminal is thus intensified by how we experience the *integrity* of the resources we access there. If, for Walter Benjamin, art lost its aura because of mass-reproduction, at the terminal, it loses it because of digitization into pixels and bytes. The technological affordance to digitally alter an existing artistic creation to fit personal preferences (or commercial interests) both endorses and attests to the profound shift in our relation to objects, environment, and self.

This experience of ephemerality naturally extends to self-presentation. Here users can also digitally alter pictures of themselves, enhance their traits, eliminate blemishes, extra weight, wrinkles, and other unflattering features. Daily. Or if they choose, they can also post complete fabrications. As users (are forced to) belong to multiplying networks, they must repeatedly invest time and energy to craft network-appropriate presentations of the self in conditions of "context collapse."[50] Afforded constant alterability and relieved of any solid commitment, the terminal self's attachment to a public 'profile' is as solid as his and her attachment to a musical playlist or an old app.

Disconnect

Terminal interactivity implements a number of disconnects between the three senses it engages (acoustic, visual, and haptic), and such disconnects intensify the experience of de-realization. Thus, even if users can become quite adept at using their mobile phones while engaged in other activities, and are found to develop new ways of integrating vision, mobility, and finger movements, for example,[51] terminal interactivity completely disconnects the habitual links between gestures and their consequences. As a simple example, the same mouse click I am using to edit this very sentence translates into an outcome as trivial as inserting a space into a text, or as inconsequential as shooting approaching warplanes in a video-game. But the very same gesture can also as easily translate into outcomes as serious as clicking 'agree' to a life-changing decision on a website, as accidentally sending a private e-mail to hundreds of recipients, or as deleting years of accumulated data from my hard drive. That similar simple gestures—however artfully executed—can trigger *instantly* widely different and often irreversibly *real* outcomes completely disrupts the commonsensical and embodied understanding that—in the physical world— gestures, their types, motions, angles, forces, frequencies, etc. materialize in corresponding and measurable effects. Here, the same gesture can translate into radically different outcomes, and different gestures can translate into the same one. Enhanced by its increasing capacity for remote control and wireless connectivity, terminal interactivity thus imposes disconnects that make it increasingly difficult to grasp what one is actually doing and what are the enduring and sometimes irreversible consequences of deceptively simple gestures that we nonchalantly type on the keyboard or click on the screen.

Terminal interactivity produces similar disconnects between visual and acoustic cues. Since we can customize the computer acoustic settings to our preferences, there is no necessary correspondence between what we see and what we hear at the terminal. Thus, for example, we can listen to Vivaldi while looking at a site devoted to Hinduism, or listen to Rap music while playing a video-game whose décor evokes medieval Japan. Any visual representation can be coupled to any sound. Such disconnects between the senses is also consequential for other aptitudes as well. As Seremetakis notes, "the memory of one sense is stored in another: that of tactility in sound, of hearing in taste, of sight in sound."[52]

Enter full screen

Thanks to its immersive quality, terminal interactivity extends the experience of ephemerality to offline modes of attention as well. While radio and television shows, books, music, meditation, sports, daydreaming, and other techniques can induce immersive experiences, those typically are—both temporally and spatially—separated from everyday life. Ubiquitous and urgent, terminal interactivity intermittently captures users' attention with instant feedback, high-definition graphics, 'noise-cancelling' sound, and sensitivity to touch.

The increasing miniaturization and portability of the terminal also enables us constant, instant, and personalized escape and immersion into this mobile and self-referential 'safe place.' If the real (offline) social situations in which we happen to find ourselves prove to be even mildly boring, challenging, or uncomfortable, it is becoming increasingly acceptable to reach for the terminal in our pockets, check in on what's happening there, and check out of what's happening here. Considering the constantly expanding universe we can access at the terminal, we can be sure we'll always find an escape. As one result, circulating through public spaces, we find ourselves in the trajectory of individuals who are completely oblivious to their environment and those who populate it. Indifferent disregard replaces Goffman's civil inattention, as they walk around, eyes glued to their terminals, expecting others to engage in the dance of 'monitoring,' 'externalization,' and 'collision avoidance' on their behalf.[53]

In contrast to several sociologists who detect a *withdrawal* from the public realm, these behaviors suggest its *appropriation*. When individuals purposefully and visibly dismiss the public realm to attend to the private terminal, and when they enforce the private terminal into the public realm, they practically transgress the boundaries that have traditionally distinguished between those two. And while social scientists typically agree that boundaries are socially constructed and that transgressing them has often prompted progressive and necessary social change, sometimes it simply does not, but invites disaster instead. In contrast to historically memorable instances where individuals collectively transgressed social boundaries to challenge political inequities, cultural sensibilities, or economic inequalities, these transgressions of the public space seem motivated simply by the desire to instantly gratify one's urges to communicate or be entertained, with complete indifference to all those present. Granted, sometimes users withdraw into the private terminal to communicate with others, and one could argue that such a behavior aims at strengthening social bonds. However, even when individuals transgress the private-public boundary to achieve such aims, they still unilaterally recode the norms of interaction in a public space that has become de facto 'personalized.'[54] Here, even Elijah Anderson's potentially redeeming "Cosmopolitan Canopy"[55] may lose its *raison d'être*, as visitors are immersed in their own private 'mental theme park,'[56] and do not have to bother acknowledging the other's existence. As Gauchet remarks, sensing a firm location in space was generative of a certain wisdom that asked us to compose with our environment and those who surround us. Today, "you can perceive those who surround you as negligible variables. You do not really see them as part of your real world."[57] The routine experience of ignoring the here and now on behalf of a constant "elsewhere" decisively transforms how we sense the physically immediate. By extracting users—mentally, emotionally, socially—from the physical context they occupy, terminal interactivity weakens the grounding forces of these physical contexts, reduces their gravity and solidity, and blurs their distinctive features. As a humorous attempt to call attention to this terminal colonization of the public space, Amsterdam offers "Wi-Fi Free" (rather than Free Wi-Fi) zones. More pragmatic, the Chinese city of Chongqing offers special pedestrian lanes for cell phone users.

Multi-purpose but mono-logical, terminal interactivity is increasingly ubiquitous and necessary to accomplish a growing number of tasks that once required distinctive devices, skills, and knowledge. Imposing the regime of urgency, reducing engagement to a few gestures that have no realistic correlates in 'real' life,[58] and normalizing a sense of ephemerality, it induces de-realization and, as I discuss below, chronic distraction.[59] According to Hartmut Rosa, our alienation from terminal devices is qualitatively different from the one described by Marx. Here the magical powers of the terminal are all too real and detached from physical reality. And although we do not understand how it functions and experience it as a constantly mutating and mysterious presence in our lives, we are fully dependent on it.

Software thinking

> Knowledge will be accumulated in "electronic banks" and transmitted directly to the human nervous system by means of coded electronic messages. There will no longer be any need of reading or learning mountains of useless information; everything will be received and registered according to the needs of the moment. There will be no need of attention or effort. What is needed will pass directly from the machine to the brain without going through consciousness.[60]

Jacques Ellul's prophetic quote introduces what I call "software thinking"—the cognitive style required by terminal interactivity, the one we adopt when we sync to its logic.[61] For Hassan, the cognitive style we adapt at the terminal prompts 'abbreviated thinking' where "the time needed to think critically and reflectively … is reduced through the combination of information overload and speed."[62] For neuroscientist Greenfield, "these technologies are infantilizing the brain into the state of small children who are attracted by buzzing noises and bright lights, who have a small attention span and who live for the moment."[63] In *The Glass Cage*, Carr discusses the sometimes catastrophic consequences of 'automation complacency' and 'automation bias'—those modes of perceptual (in)attention that kick in when we rely on the terminal to perform complex cognitive functions.[64] As he documents, the increasing use of softwares in professions such as architecture, medicine, and piloting both deskills intellectual workers and eradicates important sources of knowledge. Turkle detects other worrisome trends and quite a bit of anxiety among scientists who must increasingly rely on terminal simulations and immersion rather than on embodied and deep knowledge.[65] Below, I review two main aspects of software thinking that pertain to memory and information-management.

Auto-save

One first aspect of software thinking concerns memory. In *Delete*, Viktor Mayer-Schönberger analyzes the radical shift unleashed by the new capacities for data storage, permanence, and retrieval. As he reminds us, in previous historical periods, unless one invested purposeful efforts to remember an event, the "default" setting was to forget it. Today, the default is to (digitally) remember everything.[66] That the terminal capacities for information-management are more accurate, efficient, and rapid than those activated by human brains is clear. However, when users entrust the work of remembering to the terminal, they renounce the human functions that have traditionally been mobilized in the exercise of remembering. For example, when we try to retrieve a pertinent piece of information, our mental processes follow chains of associations that make sense to us. They make sense to us partly because the memories we produce are typically grounded in (and evoked by) embodied and multi-sensory experiences in concrete physical settings. To "make sense" refers to both sensory experiences and their interpretations.[67] However, outsourcing this process to the terminal distorts these multi-sensory and often collective endeavors beyond recognition. Removing physical sensations from memory-work disconnects body from mental processes—a disconnect that is concretized in the terminal's hard drive, the flash drive, or the Great External Drive in the Sky—The Cloud.[68] Not only are many of the events that accumulate in the terminal's memory often bereft of any contextual and embodied correlates, but we do not even need to activate our mind to access them.[69] Or rather, we need to activate our mind differently in order to retrieve a past event that—like everything else—has now been 'saved' at the terminal and encoded as 'data.' Here, contexts, associations, or triggers are irrelevant. We just type in 'search' and the terminal will help us retrieve the now-decontextualized piece of information we are looking for. As cultural critic Olivier Dyens asks, "what will happen once memories, which endow us with conscience and existence survive only in databases? How will this transform us? Today our memories almost never originate from our own decoding but are almost exclusively machine-recorded events."[70]

By outsourcing this cognitive work, we fail to activate complex processes that transform short-term memories into long-term ones. As Carr reminds us, to remember an event consists of much more than "accessing data." It is a dynamic and context-specific process that involves biochemical and anatomical transformations. And replacing that process with terminal shortcuts has consequences that extend beyond just remembering or forgetting.[71] "As we 'externalize' problem-solving and other cognitive chores to our terminals," writes Carr, "we reduce our brain's ability 'to build stable knowledge structures'—schemas that can later 'be applied in new situations'."[72] Those changes in brain functioning then inhibit the very possibility of learning new ideas and skills.[73]

At the group level, entrusting one's memory to the terminal also reduces the *collective* aspect of memory-work, as our terminal memory celebrates and confirms a very solipsistic version of (oneself in) the past and, as we'll see in the next chapter, the present and the future. For Virilio also, this outsourcing of memory has profound consequences that ripple through society and compromises social thought:

> We should, therefore, warn people against the archaic instincts of those
> who pretend to create a global realm of information without bothering

to analyse to what extent the reduction of content has destructive consequences ... They impact upon the actual creation and historical development of human beings themselves, not to mention the development of social thought.[74]

Further, when we entrust our memories to the terminal, we format them to fit its software; we encode them as digital images, sounds, words, numbers, etc. And because this encoding is digital, the information so encoded is much more vulnerable to theft, alteration, or destruction. When we outsource the *process* of remembering to the terminal, we detach this process from the somatic work it typically requires. And because our experience at the terminal is ephemeral, decontextualized, and disembodied, we may become less able to distinguish between those events that occurred at the terminal from those that occurred in concrete environments populated by physically co-present others. This experience of de-realization at the terminal may thus also contaminate the trust we have in our memory. Individuals who do not trust (or control) their memories, who are uncertain about their origins or authenticity, and who routinely experience de-realization are more vulnerable to manipulation. As Virilio put it,

> For the human memory is not merely the dead memory of the computer hard drive but the living memory of human beings. And without living human memory there is only the violence revealed by the explosion of the information bomb ...[75]

Google scholar

If terminal interactivity subverts what and how we remember, it also distorts how we manage information, a second aspect of software thinking. Philosopher Lynch expresses his concern with "Google-knowing," a type of knowledge that is significantly different from—and undermines—the much more complex, experience-based, and creative 'understanding.'[76] Unfortunately, he notes, Google-knowing is rapidly displacing other types of knowledge and the very experience of knowing. Similarly, in his research on cell phone use in France, hypermodern sociologist Jauréguiberry concludes that

> our ability to connect in real time enabled by our informational prostheses coincides with a generalized disconnect in our capacities to understand, to put in perspective, to contextualize, and to interpret the information that reaches us. Information comes in, goes out, and circulates, but it does not stop. The proliferation of information blinds us.[77]

Paradoxically, therefore, while the sheer volume of information and speed of analytic abilities enabled by the terminal should enhance users' capacity to understand many topics at a most sophisticated level, the opposite obtains.

We may have access to more information and faster than at any other time in the history of our species, but we are decreasingly capable of making sense of it, let alone, evaluate, integrate, and use it. As Andrejevic sees it, the analysis of gargantuan volumes of 'big data' yields correlations and predictions, but rarely explanations.[78]

Relatedly, even though reading a text at the terminal will prompt less engagement, understanding, and remembering than reading it on paper, Google wants to digitize everything that's been written.[79] As Ebert notes,

> We are forced ... to trade off a diversity of media sources—magazines, newspapers, etc.—for only one kind of media: digital. The disappearance of diversity, especially of media, is never a good thing, for in this case, it amounts to a massive cultural impoverishment. As a result of the elimination of choices, we are increasingly forced to rely more and more on the Internet in order to get access to our media, our news and our information, articles, essays, reviews, etc., which is only *one* means of purveying such media and arguably not even the best.[80]

At my university library, for example an increasing number of books are now only available as e-books. In addition to inducing a shallower engagement, many of these e-books that I download on my terminal are accessible *for only two weeks*, after which they magically become unavailable.[81] This curious management of intellectual resources not only betrays a poor understanding of how academics actually work with texts, it also illustrates how terminals present information to users and how users attend to it. As research suggests, more and more scholars cite less and less articles, and what they cite is predicated by self-fulfilling search engines that, as Carr notes, "give precedence to popularity and recency over diversity of opinion, rigor of argument or quality of expression."[82] Whether and how scholars actually read the articles they cite is also notorious. As a study conducted by the British Library finds, users spend an average of four minutes on an e-book. Another research report that 60 percent of serious scholars do not read more than three pages of an e-journal, and 65 percent of them never come back for a second look. This same report also mentions reading patterns such as "horizontal bouncing" across texts, and Nicholas Carr reports on an F-shaped reading pattern.[83] Discussing the quality of this nascent 'scholarship,' Rosa also notes other trends:

> The speed and succession of conferences and articles are so high, and— even worse than the number of articles—the number of published books and journals is so excessive that those who write and express themselves in this era dominated by the 'publish or perish' motto have a hard time finding enough time to correctly develop their arguments, while those who read and listen are lost on a jungle of half-baked and repetitive publications and presentations ... I am convinced that today, at least in the social sciences and the humanities, it has become very difficult to find a

consensus on the force of conviction of the best arguments. In contrast, we find ourselves caught in a mad and uncontrollable race towards always more publications, conferences and research projects whose success is based on personal networks rather than on the force of argumentation.[84]

Relying on software thinking, the terminal self might be rapidly losing the capacity to read a book from start to finish, to engage in continuous reading, and to appreciate long dénouement. No longer seeking to immerse oneself in a text, attune to the author's voice, and enter the worlds created by words, the terminal self scans a text to locate and pluck out those bits of information that seem immediately relevant for the task at hand. Such a mode of cognitive attention does not enable deep understanding or critical thinking. As Katherine Hayles reports, "recent studies indicate that hyper-reading not only requires different reading strategies than close reading but also may be involved with changes in brain architecture that makes close-reading difficult to achieve."[85] Carr also notes that in the same way that the dissemination of reading and writing deeply affected our brain structure and functioning, interacting with the terminal literally *produces different brains,*[86] and does so surprisingly rapidly:

> It's not just that we tend to us the Net regularly, even obsessively: It's that the Net delivers precisely the kind of sensory and cognitive stimuli— repetitive, intensive, interactive, addictive—that have been show to result in strong and rapid alterations in brain circuitry and functions ... The Net also provides a high-speed system for delivering responses and rewards—"positive reinforcements," in psychological terms—which encourage the repetition of both physical and mental actions.[87]

The information that coalesces as 'Google-knowing' is produced by others and is constantly manipulated by a wide variety of organizations and interests. And as users increasingly defer to the terminal to find information about pretty much any topic, as Google-knowing supplants other—and decreasingly valued—forms of knowing, the terminal self's capacity to *understand* phenomena is undermined.[88] French sociologist Jacques Ellul also decried a near future whereby

> The intelligentsia will no longer be a model, a conscience, or an animat-ing intellectual spirit for the group, even in the sense of performing a critical function. They will be the servants, the most conformist imagin-able, of the instruments of technique ... And education will no longer be an unpredictable and exciting adventure in human enlightenment, but an exercise in conformity and an apprenticeship to whatever gadgetry is useful in a technical world.[89]

In addition, as the information displayed at the terminal is likely to be increas-ingly personalized, and as users lack solid epistemic principles with which to evaluate it, they can quickly lose the capacity to share vital information, and to put it to pragmatic and ethical use. Thus, a recent research conducted at Stanford University concludes that students have a "dismaying inability" to distinguish between fake and real news,[90] and this affliction is not limited to students. Research reports that Facebook users are more likely to share fake (but dramatic) news than real ones, a finding which is especially worrisome when one considers that 44 percent of adult Americans get their news from Facebook,[91] and 62 percent from social media.[92] Recent concern about the epidemic of fake news appearing on social media since the 2016 election and, one suspects, before that, suggests that this confusion is occurring faster than we can understand or control, and that it impacts increasingly deeper and serious levels of societal functioning.

Edit search criteria

Syncing to terminal interactivity, outsourcing cognitive tasks, and resorting to software thinking have been found to inhibit creative association, to reduce randomness and serendipity, to decontextualize, to promote a passive learning disposition, to activate incomplete knowledge, and to favor hyper-focus rather than general knowledge and synthesis.[93] As Turkle puts it, the terminal gives us a "new way *not* to think."[94] And beyond the degradation and stunting of specific cognitive competencies, software thinking also alters their integration and interdependencies, thereby re-designing our brain architecture.[95] In so doing, it reinforces our dependence on the terminal, which then prompts more outsourcing, in an increasingly downward cognitive spiral. We are unlikely to notice this degradation because—among other reasons—as long as we follow the rules of software thinking, the personalized terminal rewards us. It validates us as skillful, efficient, productive, and powerful. We are also unlikely to notice it because, as Google-knowing is increasingly supplanting other forms of knowing, we have diminishing alternative models with which to gauge our cognitive decline. For Lynch, software thinking does not only degrade cognitive functions, but it threatens the very possibility of democracy.[96]

In sum, interactivity, the first terminal default setting, is not only unique in terms of combining a number of novel and disorienting features. It is also, and especially, unique because, in contrast to many other technologies that "act back" on users but that users can avoid in their everyday life, terminal interactivity is becoming increasingly necessary and ubiquitous. We no longer have much choice but to sync to it, multiple times a day, for a growing number of functions, on the go, and across different devices. Terminal interactivity is also unique because, in contrast to other technologies that can act back, the terminal does so *intelligently*. This form of interactivity is not always predictable and adjusts itself to us, remembers what we do, can advise use, anticipate what we want, etc. Accordingly, perhaps new sets of questions social constructionists and actor-network theorists might want to consider is not necessarily whether a technology under consideration is human or not, but the degree to which it is intelligent and/or autonomous. I develop this topic in the "Submit" chapter.

Notes

1 Vannini (2009).
2 Woodward (2009), 68–69.
3 Carr (2011), 211.
4 Hassan (2012), 90.
5 Hassan (2009), 134.
6 Baym (2010), 152.
7 Bodford, Kwan, and Sobota (2017), 320.
8 The exception is going off the grid. In this case, however, the decision to completely disconnect has enormous consequences for one's employability or ability to access most essential resources necessary for sheer functioning in this society.
9 Greenfield (2017).
10 Ibid.
11 Parisi (2008).
12 Franks (2003), 624.
13 Ibid.
14 Gabriele (2008), 523.
15 Tisseron (2008).
16 Carr (2015), 137.
17 Ebert (2011), 93–101.
18 Ibid.
19 Quoted in Carr (2015), 132.
20 Carr (2015), 137.
21 Seremetakis (1994), 90.
22 Wajcman (2008), 72.
23 Derks and Bakker (2010).
24 Turkle (2011).
25 Baym (2010), 4.
26 Jauréguiberry (2014), 32.
27 Rushkoff (2011), 35–36.
28 Zerubavel (1985).
29 Turkle (2009), p. 8.
30 See Rosa (2012). Physical consumption refers to the discarding of an object when it can no longer be used. Moral consumption refers to the discarding of objects who are still useful but no longer fashionable.
31 Rojek (2004), 306–307.
32 Greenfield (2017), op. cit.
33 Gillath, in press.
34 Aubert (2008a), 29.
35 Tisseron (2008).
36 Rosa (2012).
37 Rosa (2012), 119.
38 The Snapchat app—which enables users to send pictures or videos that disappear in ten seconds—perhaps best illustrates this condition.
39 Rosa (2012), 177.
40 Rainie and Anderson (2017).
41 The invention and promotion of the 'cloud' is the perfect illustration of this ephemerality and immateriality. With all one's information stored in a virtual space, it is not the particular terminal device one uses that matters, but the storage

capacity one owns, the speed and ease of access, and the security systems protecting it.

42 Bardhi and Eckhardt (2012).

43 Fuchs (2017), 147.

44 See especially Bauman's discussions of waste in *Liquid Life* (2005).

45 Lipovetsky (2006).

46 While most commercial companies are still relying on human beings to deliver these commodities to our doors, certain companies are considering relying on drones to do so.

47 Unless you buy the entire album.

48 At the same time, urban legends also urged us to play some of them counterclockwise (Beatles) or in conjunction with other texts (Pink Floyd) in order to access a secret layer of meanings.

49 As Ebert (2011) shows, digital photography corrupts manual photography in parallel ways as well.

50 Marwick and boyd (2010).

51 Richardson and Third (2009).

52 Seremetakis (1994), 28.

53 Collet and Marsh (1981).

54 Berman (2006).

55 Anderson (2011).

56 Berman (2000), 49.

57 Gauchet (2005), 298.

58 For example, in real life, pressing on a plastic key cannot erase an entire folder of scholarly articles. As another example, in real life, pressing on a plastic key cannot, materially, send a short message simultaneously to 125 people dispersed across the planet.

59 See Hassan (2012); Jackson (2009).

60 Ellul (1964), 432.

61 It goes without saying that terminal interactivity prompts physical and sensory adaptations as well. See for example, Vannini, Waskul, and Gottschalk (2011).

62 Hassan (2009), 98 and 120.

63 Quoted in Keen (2012), 69.

64 Carr (2015).

65 Turkle (2009).

66 Mayer-Schönberger (2011).

67 Vannini, Waskul, and Gottschalk (2011).

68 In spite of its ephemeral quality, The Cloud refers to real buildings, machines, electric currents, cables, etc.

69 This statement refers mainly to those terminal experiences where users read texts or view images, and excludes those experiences one can have when interacting in virtual settings or on platforms that enable users to see and hear each other, when playing some video-games, playing with a Wii, and others.

70 Dyens (2001), 36.

71 Mayer-Schönberger (2011).

72 Carr (2011), 216.

73 Carr (2011), 191–192.

74 Virilio, Kittler, and Armitage (1999), 90.

75 Ibid.

76 Lynch (2016).

77 Jauréguiberry (2014), 48.

78 Andrejevic (2013).

79 Carr (2011), 90.

80 Ebert (2011), 12.

81 The most recent one I downloaded is available for only 24 hours.
82 Carr (2015).
83 As described by Carr (2011, 134–135), "F-reading" refers to an F-like eye movement when reading whereby the reader examines the top of the text, then scrolls down and reads a bit in the middle, and then slides down to the end.
84 Rosa (2012), 74.
85 Hayles (2012).
86 Carr (2011), 120.
87 Carr (2011), 116–117.
88 Lynch (2016).
89 Ellul (1964), 348.
90 Domonoske (2016).
91 *New York Times* Editorial Board (2016). Of course, 'fake news' has become the leitmotif of the 2016 elections and the current state of political chaos.
92 Rainie, Anderson, and Albright (2017).
93 Carr (2015).
94 Turkle (2011), 240.
95 Turkle (2011); see also Roberts (2014).
96 Lynch (2016).

References

Anderson, Elijah. 2011. *The Cosmopolitan Canopy: Race and Civility in Everyday Life.* New York: W. W. Norton & Co.

Andrejevic, Mark. 2013. *Infoglut: How Too Much Information Is Changing the Way We Think and Know.* New York: Routledge.

Aubert, Nicole. 2008a. "Violence du Temps et Pathologies Hypermodernes." *Cliniques Méditerranéennes* 78: 23–38.

Bardhi, Fleura and Giana M. Eckhardt. 2012. "Access-Based Consumption: The Case of Car Sharing." *Journal of Consumer Research* 39(4): 881–898.

Bauman, Zygmunt. 2005. *Liquid Life.* Cambridge, UK: Polity.

Baym, Nancy K. 2010. *Personal Connections in the Digital Age.* Cambridge, UK: Polity.

Berman, Morris. 2000. *The Twilight of American Culture.* New York: W. W. Norton & Co.

Berman, Morris. 2006. *Dark Ages America: The Final Phase of Empire.* New York: W. W. Norton & Co.

Bodford, Jessica E., Virginia S. Y. Kwan, and David S. Sobota. 2017. "Fatal Attractions: Attachment to Smartphones Predicts Anthropomorphic Beliefs and Dangerous Behaviors." *Cyberpsychology, Behavior, and Social Networking,* 20(5): 320–326.

Carr, Nicholas. 2011. *The Shallows: What the Internet is Doing to Our Brains.* New York: W. W. Norton & Co.

Carr, Nicholas. 2015. *The Glass Cage: Where Automation is Taking Us.* London: The Bodley Head.

Collet, Peter and Peter Marsh. 1981. "Patterns of Public Behavior: Collision Avoidance on a Pedestrian Crossing." pp. 199–218 in *Nonverbal Communication, Interaction, and Gesture,* Adam Kendon et al. (eds.). The Hague: Mouton.

Derks, Daantje and Arnold B. Bakker. 2010. "The Impact of E-Mail Communication on Organizational Life." *Cyberpsychology: Journal of Psychosocial Research on Cyberspace* 4(1). Retrieved December 12, 2013. file://localhost/(http://cyberpsychology.eu:view.php%3Fcisloclanku=2010052401&article=1).

Domonoske, Camilia. 2016. "Students Have 'Dismaying' Inability To Tell Fake News From Real, Study Finds." KNPR. Retrieved November 23, 2016. www.npr.org/sections/thetwo-way/2016/11/23/503129818/study-finds-students-have-dismaying-inability-to-tell-fake-news-from-real.

Dyens, Ollivier. 2001. *Metal and Flesh: Technology Takes Over*. Cambridge, MA: MIT Press.

Ebert, John David. 2011. *The New Media Invasion: Digital Technologies and the World They Unmake*. Jefferson, NC: McFarlane.

Ellul, Jacques. 1964. *The Technological Society*. New York: Alfred A. Knopf.

Franks, David. 2003. "Mutual Interests, Different Lenses: Current Neuroscience and Symbolic Interaction." *Symbolic Interaction* 26(4): 613–630.

Fuchs, Christian. 2017. *Social Media: A Critical Introduction*. Los Angeles: Sage.

Gabriele Alex. 2008. "A Sense of Belonging and Exclusion: 'Touchability' and 'Untouchability' in Tamil Nadu." *Ethnos*, 73(4): 523–543.

Gauchet, Marcel. "Vers une Mutation Anthropologique?" pp. 290–301 in *L'Individu Hypermoderne*, Nicole Aubert (ed.). Toulouse: Érès.

Gillath, Omri. In press. *Adult Attachment: A Concise Introduction to Theory and Research*. Washington D.C.: Academic Press.

Greenfield, Adam. 2017. *Radical Technologies: The Design of Everyday Life*. Verso. Available at: https://longreads.com/2017/06/13/a-sociology-of-the-smartphone/. Retrieved June 14, 2017.

Hassan, Robert. 2009. *Empires of Speed: Time and the Acceleration of Politics and Society*. Leiden: Brill.

Hassan, Robert. 2012. *The Age of Distraction*. New Brunswick: Transactions.

Hayles, N. Katherine. 2012. *How We Think: Digital Media and Contemporary Technogenesis*. University of Chicago Press.

Jackson, Maggie. 2009. *Distracted: The Erosion of Attention and the Coming Dark Age*. New York: Prometheus.

Jauréguiberry, Francis. 2014. "La Déconnection aux Technologies de Communication." *La Découverte-Réseaux* 186(4): 15–49.

Keen, Andrew. 2012. *Digital Vertigo: How Today's Online Social Revolution is Dividing, Diminishing, and Disorienting Us*. New York: St. Martin Griffin.

Lipovetsky, Gilles. 2006. *Le Bonheur Paradoxal: Essai sur la Société d'Hyperconsommation*. Paris: Gallimard.

Lynch, Michael Patrick. 2016. *The Internet of Us: Knowing More and Understanding Less in the Age of Big Data*. New York: Liveright.

Marwick, Alice and danah boyd. 2010. "I Tweet Honestly, I Tweet Passionately: Twitter Users, Context Collapse, and the Imagined Audience." *New Media & Society*. 13(1): 114–133.

Mayer-Schonberger, Viktor. 2011. *Delete: The Virtue of Forgetting in the Digital Age*. Princeton, NJ: Princeton University Press.

New York Times Editorial Board. 2016. "Facebook and the Digital Virus Called Fake News" November 19. Retrieved November 20, 2016. www.nytimes.com/2016/11/20/opinion/sunday/facebook-and-the-digital-virus-called-fake-news.html?hpw&rref=sunday-review&action=click&pgtype=Homepage&module=well-region&region=bottom-well&WT.nav=bottom-well.

Parisi, David. 2008. "'Fingerbombing,' or 'Touching is Good': The Cultural Construction of Technologized Touch." *Senses & Society* 3(3): 307–327.

Rainie, Lee and Janna Anderson. 2017. "Code-Dependent: Pros and Cons of the Algorithm Age." Pew Research Center, February 2017. Available at: www.pewinternet. org/2017/02/08/code-dependent-pros-and-cons-of-the-algorithm-age.

Rainie, Lee, Janna Anderson, and Jonathan Albright. 2017. "The Future of Free Speech, Trolls, Anonymity, and Fake News Online." Pew Research Center, March 2017. Available at: www.pewinternet.org/2017/03/29/the-future-of-free-speech-trolls-anonymity-and-fake-news-online/. Downloaded June 9, 2017.

Richardson, Ingrid and Amanda Third. 2009. "Cultural Phenomenology and the Material Culture of Mobile Media." pp. 145–156 in *Material Culture and Technology in Every Day: Ethnographic Approaches*, Phillip Vannini (ed.). New York: Peter Lang.

Roberts, Paul. 2014. *The Impulse Society: America in the Age of Instant Gratification*. New York: Bloomsberry.

Rojek, Chris, 2004. "The Consumerist Syndrome in Contemporary Society: An Interview with Zygmunt Bauman" *Journal of Consumer Culture* 4(3): 291–312.

Rosa, Hartmut. 2012. *Aliénation et Accélération: Vers une Théorie Critique de la Modernité Tardive*. Paris: La Découverte.

Rushkoff, Douglas. 2011. *Program or be Programmed: Ten Commands for a Digital Age*. Berkeley, CA: Soft Skull Press.

Seremetakis, Nadia C. 1994. "The Memory of the Senses, Part I: Marks of the Transitory." pp. 1–18 in *The Senses Still: Perception and Memory as Material Culture in Modernity*, Nadia C. Seremetakis (ed.). Boulder: Westview.

Tisseron, Serge. 2008. *Virtuel, Mon Amour: Penser, Aimer, Souffrir à l'Ére des Nouvelles Technologies*. Paris: Albin Michel.

Turkle, Sherry. 2009. *Simulation and Its Discontents*. Cambridge, MA: MIT Press.

Turkle, Sherry. 2011. *Alone Together: Why We Demand More of Technology and Less of Each Other*. New York: Basic Books.

Vannini, Phillip (ed.). 2009. *Material Culture and Technology in Every Day: Ethnographic Approaches*. New York: Peter Lang.

Vannini, Phillip, Dennis Waskul, and Simon Gottschalk. 2011. *The Senses in Self, Society, and Culture: A Sociology of the Senses*. New York: Routledge.

Virilio, Paul, Friedrich Kittler, and John Armitage. 1999. "The Information Bomb: A Conversation." *Angelaki: Journal of the Theoretical Humanities*, 4(2): 81–90. http:// dx.doi.org/10.1080/09697259908572036.

Wajcman, Judy. 2008. "Life in the Fast Lane? Towards a Sociology of Technology and Time." *The British Journal of Sociology* 59(1): 59–77.

Woodward, Ian. 2009. "Material Culture and Narrative: Fusing Myth, Materiality, and Meaning." pp. 59–72 in *Material Culture and Technology in Every Day: Ethnographic Approaches*, Phillip Vannini (ed.). New York: Peter Lang.

Zerubavel, Eviatar. 1985. *Hidden Rhythms: Schedules and Calendars in Social Life*. Berkeley, CA: University of California Press.

4 Personalize

Although our enforced interactions with the terminal should prompt spirited resistance, it does not. On the contrary, we love our terminal. We never leave home without it and we bring it with us wherever we go. We look at it with focused attention; we interrupt whatever we are doing and turn toward it full of expectations whenever it vibrates or rings. We talk to it, listen to it, and decorate it. We conspire with it and entrust our secrets to it. We rely on it to remember information we deem important, and consult it when making important decisions. Its mere presence in a setting already transforms interaction.[1] We feel lost without it and violated when others look at it without our permission. It can sometimes betray us, and can shake our world to its very foundations when it stops functioning or when we lose it.

In contrast to its older versions, today's terminal provides us with hitherto undreamed of opportunities to customize our experience with it. Cultural critics of the internet industry consider this affordance as *the* essential innovation that launched Web 3.0—the third internet revolution. Initially introduced in 2009 to improve the performance of the Google search engine, this ability to have a personalized 'search' experience at the terminal has rapidly evolved and spread to many terminal functions. Like the other default terminal settings I discuss in this book, personalization prompts a distinctive relation to the terminal that normalizes and amplifies similar trends that scholars have noted in hypermodern institutions, in the realms of everyday life, in interpersonal relations, and in subjectivity.

For example, Gilles Lipovetsky defines the current moment as the third phase in the evolution of capitalist consumption. In contrast to former periods, today's 'hyper-individualistic turbo-consumers' no longer purchase commodities and services to satisfy objective needs, to convey distinction from other social classes, or identification with their own classes. As "consumption for oneself has replaced consumption for the other," they purchase commodities and services that gratify sensuous, psychological, and affective desires instead.[2] As he explains,

> we want objects to live with, not to display them; we do not buy commodities because they enable us to show off and establish our social

status, but because they gratify us emotionally, physically, sensually, and because they entertain us. We expect the commodities we buy to enable us to be more independent, more mobile, to have new sensuous experiences, to improve our quality of life, to keep us young and healthy.[3]

In Lipovetsky's analysis, the very commodities that define the current stage of consumption concretely materialize this individualistic-hedonistic orientation. Smart phones, tablets, laptops, high-tech 'noise-cancelling' headphones, virtual reality headsets, fit-bits bracelets, personal music players, and iWatches all cater to and validate self-indulgent, mobile, and hyper-connected subjects who want to gratify their needs however, whenever, and wherever they feel like it. With or without others' participation. Or rather, as I develop in the next two chapters, requiring a certain *type* of participation. Symptomatically, even the two sides of a conjugal bed can now be individually personalized for firmness, incline, and temperature. Or, as the female voices on a *Korea Air* TV commercial ad seductively sing to potential travelers, "It's all about you." Focusing especially on smart phones, Ebert notes:

> Only in an age in which the private microsphere of the individual has become the basic elementary socio-cosmological unit, could cell phone technology exist. Indeed, the technology itself actually makes the hidden ontology visible. We have cell phones because each of us is now a world-island, a cosmos-in-miniature, unto himself and the cell phone, correspondingly, is a technological outgrowth made possible by this basic ontological fact of the status of the human individual who now exists "outside" of any protective macropshere.[4]

Beyond the sphere of consumption, Lipovetsky also calls our attention to the personalization trends that are visible in all "the new mechanisms of human resources and personnel management." They are also obvious in broader cultural shifts, such as:

> autonomy, a search for quality of life, passion of the personality, cult of participation and expression, a new form of individualism, a psychological sensibility of destabilized tolerance, a focus on one's own emotional self-fulfillment, a hunger for youth, sports, and rhythm, and a collective narcissism that prompts individuals to develop networks and connections to hyper-specialized micro-groups that commit to miniature causes and the demand for special recognition.[5]

And thanks to increasingly responsive technologies, neo-liberal citizens who can afford it can easily gratify such desires through concrete everyday practices that are becoming increasingly normalized and encouraged:

> We fine-tune our moods with pharmaceuticals and classic rock. Craft our meals around our allergies and ideologies. Customize our bodies with

cross-training, with ink and metal, with surgery and wearable technologies. We can choose a vehicle to express our hipness or hostility. We can move to a neighborhood that matches our social values, find a news outlet that mirrors our politics, create a social network that "likes" everything we say or post. With each transaction and upgrade, each choice and click, life moves closer to us, and the world becomes *our* world.[6]

For Lipovetsky, this "society of hyperconsumption where everybody feels entitled to the best and the most beautiful"[7] is nothing less than a "sociological mutation."[8] As Castel also notes:

Hypermodern individuals believe they are hyper-independent to the point of feeling free from all responsibility and free from having to account for their choices and behaviors ... There is a sort of inflation of individualism and subjectivity which is difficult to reconcile with social life, and with adhering to collective systems of regulation which are essential to life in any society.[9]

Because the terminal is rapidly becoming the main conduit for information-gathering, entertainment, interaction, and self-presentation, it seems critical to assess the effects of this personalization, both at the terminal and away from it. I first distinguish between three levels of terminal personalization, and consider the sorts of psychosocial dispositions they reward.

MySpace

At a first and concrete level, personalization refers to our ability to customize the very appearance and some functioning of the terminal. We can, for example, decide on the number, types, organization, location, and animations of the icons that populate our screen. We configure the terminal's brightness, color intensity, screensavers, background images, themes, windows' sizes, sounds, and haptic sensitivity. We choose the speed of clicking, scrolling, and tracking of the mouse. We pick the shape, color, size, and design of our virtual keyboard. We select the fonts, assign the shortcuts, and set the toolbars. We schedule certain operations and we program our 'security' and 'privacy' parameters. On all our terminals, our 'preferences' become the rule and become concretized into a visible (virtual) reality that we can share, comment on, and continuously alter. As the famous Apple motto reminded potential iPod customers, "it does not express you; it *is* you." In addition, and under the constant threat of hacking, we are encouraged to personalize our terminal even more by encoding secret passwords, sweeping patterns, or fingerprints that will protect it. Of course, although generous, this affordance to personalize the physical aspects of the terminal is not limitless. It is still encoded by certain rules to which we must submit, and which we cannot change, at least not without a great deal of specialized knowledge. Still, this palpable ability to personalize the look of our terminal constitutes a profound revolution in our relation to objects. No other technological device of its category enables it.

Filter content

The personalization of our experience at the terminal extends to a second and more worrisome level than the esthetic one. Tripped by enigmatic algorithms, the terminal daily nudges us to personalize not just its look and feel, but also its content. And even if we resist this temptation, the terminal will autonomously expose us to some type of content but not others. Through both explicit and implicit messages that relentlessly pop up on the windows we happen to be browsing, the terminal 'recommends' newspapers we'd probably like to read, music we'd probably like to hear, food we'd probably like to taste, places we'd probably like to visit, people we'd probably like to 'friend,' and political causes we'd probably like to contribute to. In addition, if we are offended, bored, or distressed by any type of content, we can easily report it, delete it, avoid it, and filter all future similar ones. Unsurprisingly, this disposition also replicates in our treatment of the real people we encounter at the terminal. On social media sites, e-mail, instant messaging, and other platforms, we can dismiss, block, ignore, un-friend, and crop out of our lives those who have displeased us, those whose attitudes, poor taste, or belief system offend us, and those who simply bore us. It is quite telling that Facebook started as a college site where students could rapidly rate and dismiss their peers on the basis of their physical attractiveness. As we increasingly personalize our terminal experience and as it records our choices, mirrors those back to us, and continuously fine-tunes them, we withdraw into what Eli Pariser calls a 'filter bubble.' As he notes,

> Ultimately, the proponents of personalization offer a vision of a custom-tailored world, every facet of which fits us perfectly. It's a cozy place, populated by our favorite people and things and ideas … If we never click on the articles about cooking, or gadgets, or the world outside our country's borders, they simply fade away … We're never bored. We're never annoyed. Our media is a perfect reflection of our interests and desires.[10]

We have probably always sought to develop a comfortable filter bubble that validates our opinions and confirms our worldview. But, writes Pariser, there are three significant differences between those more traditional filter bubbles and the terminal one. First, we're alone in the terminal bubble. It exists for us and only for us. Second, we no longer have a choice, but are forced to live in it. Third, as the algorithms follow their own logic, we no longer control it. "The belief that one's view of reality is the only reality is the most dangerous of all delusions," wrote Paul Watzlawick. Yet, the terminal's increasingly precise algorithms sanction this very delusion by producing an 'endless you-loop.'

As Pariser warns, however, as we adjust the terminal to our self, we simultaneously adjust our self to the terminal.[11] And the self-validating and seemingly harmless desire to personalize the terminal look and content then extends to our relation to the world itself, writes Roberts: "To personalize is, in effect, to reject the world 'as is,' and instead to insist on bending it to our preferences ...."[12] For hypermodern psychologist Tisseron, terminal technologies usher in the *Society of Denial*: "With the new technologies, everything becomes organized so as to be able to ignore what one does not want to know ... The role of the virtual sphere will be to normalize this refusal."[13]

As Bauman also suggests, this orientation replicates in our relationships with real and co-present others as well,[14] a trend that symbolic interactionists should find particularly interesting. Social psychologists of various stripes have long established that the ability to self-reflect from an increasingly complex, abstract, diverse, different, and distant other's perspective is key to mental-moral evolution, to emotional and social intelligence, and—more generally—to sanity.

Perhaps unsurprisingly, while the terminal has multiplied the number of people with whom users can potentially interact and self-reflect, Sherry Turkle's research suggests that today's youth are both decreasingly capable of role-taking, and of finding much value in the ability to do so.[15] But personalization inhibits role-taking abilities among adult users too. They complicate its performance, reduce the opportunities to do so well, and impoverish the mechanisms by which they acquire and develop it. Since terminals provide us with a personalized access to literally the universe whenever we want to and wherever we happen to be at, they also position us at the omnipotent, omnipresent, and mobile center of our high-def private 'socio-mental space.' Roberts notes that

> moment to moment, we have the potential to make our leisure time ... into a sequence of personal, personalizing experiences in which various smart technologies filter out the stressful and the mundane so we can get on with our real job, which, apparently, is self-expression.[16]

Celebrating 'profound self-involvement'[17] and deforming the meaning of interaction to an absurd caricature, this personalization of content limits those imaginative capacities that have always been at the heart of mature social beingness. As Lipovetsky put it most succinctly: "personalization creates emptiness in Technicolor."[18]

On a different level, this type of personalization also presents worrisome political implications. In mass society, politicians seek to mobilize individuals by communicating their messages in mass media texts such as speeches printed in newspapers, broadcast on TV, movies, or the radio. The critical analysis of these speeches often reveals the *unifying* ideologies they convey. Because political leaders seek to convert heterogeneous—and sometimes dispersed—audience members into a homogenized and obedient mass, they must pitch their speeches accordingly. They must address every individual as a potential soldier, comrade, pioneer, or citizen of a noble collective endeavor, and transform isolated "I's" into a heroic "we." Speakers can enhance the persuasive impact of those unifying texts when they communicate them "live" to physically co-present individuals at mass rallies. In these conditions, how audience members interpret the content of the messages they hear is mediated by the visible, kinetic, and audible reactions they observe among co-present others. In so doing, audience members evaluate those messages' relative importance, emotional charge, level of consensus, etc., and react accordingly.[19]

Like traditional mass media technologies, the terminal also communicates and reproduces ideological assumptions. By design, it disseminates implicit 'lessons' about how to think, how to evaluate others and how to relate to them; lessons about what matters and where one fits in the scheme of things. One meaningful difference, however, is that at the terminal, we no longer attend to these lessons as members of a mass audience, let alone a community. Rather, we attend to them as isolated receptors of a continuous communication stream whose content and style is personalized with increasing precision to who we think we are—or ought to be. Discussing the case of political candidates, Andrejevic notes that

> instead of tailoring a general message designed to maximize common appeal and minimize offense, the goal is to target individuals and groups based on key motivating issues—to provide not a generalized, blurry portrait of the candidate, but a customized high resolution perspective portrait that can be modified to meet the interests and concerns of specific audiences.[20]

Studying current trends in voter surveillance, Colin Bennett also finds that, in light of the ever-increasing amount of information political parties can access, they no longer "convey their messages to broad geographic or demographic communities." Instead, they rely on "the micro-targeting of more precise segments of the electorate" and communicate tailored messages "through the individual's preferred communication medium."[21] As Roberts also finds, the terminal personalization of the political discourse and the disappearance of challenging viewpoints lead to the polarization of the political spectrum. It encourages extreme positions and undermines the very possibility of dialogue.[22] The recent debates about "fact-checking" political speeches, living in a "post-truth" era, and "alternative facts" unfortunately support President Obama's contention that this personalized filter bubble is one of the three main threats to contemporary democracy.[23]

However, as scholar Judith Donnath suggests, such transformations can be more subtle:

> In the next few years we are likely to face a generation of social robots designed to persuade us. Some will be motivating us at our own

request—weight-loss and exercise cheerleaders, for example. But most will be guided by others, whose intentions for influencing us are guided not by an altruistic concern with our well-being, but by goals such as getting us to buy more of what they are selling. Such goals are often not in our own best interest ... [The new social robot] will sustain its user in a highly personalized, adaptive, long-term relationship through social and emotional engagement—in the spirit of technological 'Jiminy Cricket'— that provides the right message, at the right time, in the right way to gently nudge its user to make smarter decisions.[24]

What remains unclear, however, is the definition of this personalized 'smarter,' its authors, and the ideological assumptions it articulates.

Instant download

"All the Power You Want. All Day Long," promises the new MacBook Air commercial ad. *"Rule the Air,"* a printed *Verizon* commercial ad exhorts young viewers. Whether we want to access our GPS, listen to music, play a video-game, send someone a joke, or launch a meditation app, we expect that the terminal will immediately respond to our desires. Instantly, constantly, and non-judgmentally. Following in Siri's electronic footsteps, the terminal is no longer just acutely sensitive to our touch, it can now also attend to our spoken commands, obey them, and is well on its way to anticipate them. At a third level therefore, the very *functioning* of the terminal also promotes the experience of personalization by normalizing the delusional and quite regressive expectation of constant individual attention and instant gratification. To wit, a recent study reports that we expect a webpage to load at— literally—the blink of an eye, and random delays in our ability to connect or download that were routine a mere 15 years ago have now become intolerable. Assessing the sources of *The Impulsive Society*, Roberts finds that "much of what Apple and most other purveyors of personal technology, from Google to Microsoft to Facebook, are selling really is ... the ability to generate the highest level of momentary pleasure for the least effort."[25] For Eriksen, terminal technologies normalize what he calls the 'tyranny of the moment'—a disposition "which demands unmediated, instant gratification, which promises ever new and more exciting moments, and which militates against the values associated with history, connectedness and duration."[26] As Bauman also notes, the main characteristic and supreme value of the society of consumers is its historically unique promise to deliver "happiness in *earthly life*, and happiness *here* and *now* and in *every* successive 'now'; in short, an *instant* and perpetual happiness."[27]

Viewed in this perspective, Elliot Rodgers' murderous rantings take on a different dimension. On May 23, 2014, Elliot Rodgers—a 23 year old heterosexual white man—went on a killing spree in Isla Vista, the student community adjacent to the University of California Santa Barbara. Before committing his crime, he posted—on YouTube—a video titled "Elliot Rodger's Retribution," where he explained the motivations for the crimes he was about to commit. Beyond the venomous and virulent accusations of being denied love, acceptance, validation, etc., his grievance at being prevented from gratifying his sexual urges at will deserves, I believe, special attention. In a society that has benefitted from a modicum of sexual liberation in the wake of the 1960s, in a society where pornography is easier to get than a pack of cigarettes, the ability to have consensual and non-commercial sex with a woman is still, it seems, an important experience young heterosexual men must successfully complete in order to establish masculinity, a sense of self-worth, or at least, of normalcy among their peers.[28] Elliot Rodgers' decision to destroy himself and attractive young women rather than work through the reality of delayed—or improbable—gratification is perhaps an extreme manifestation of a hyper-consumerist sense of entitlement. Entitlement for the immediate satisfaction of one's desires, for validation, and for personalized attention. Because the gratification of these desires typically necessitates others' willing collaboration, this sense of entitlement that is so cultivated by the very functioning of the terminal also normalizes an exploitative and rather infantile understanding of human relations.

As Lipovetsky notes "Homo consumans becomes allergic to the slightest wait,"[29] and if Elliot Rodgers' reactions are indeed extreme, milder manifestations become increasingly common in other niches of everyday life than libidinal urges, consumption, or 'frictionless' access to online services. Nervously competing for 'constant and partial attention' while routinely being 'paused,'[30] terminal selves are especially likely to expect this sense of entitlement to be promptly gratified whenever they feel like communicating whatever thoughts, emotions, or desires are crossing their minds.[31] For example, Liz, a graduate student, explains:

> It's like I am driving to my boy-friend's house and texting him: "On my way. Will be there in 5 minutes," and he does not answer. So I check my phone and I'm getting angrier and angrier because I don't see any response. So I send him another text "u there?" Still no answer. Then another message. Then I feel like smashing my phone on the ground.

Jerry, another graduate student echoes this orientation:

> Yesterday I sent an email to that guy and was waiting for his answer, waiting, waiting. I got so mad, I felt like getting into my car and driving to his house and scream at him "I sent you an email three fucking hours ago, why am I still waiting?"

As Bugeja reminds us, "Technology may function 'on demand' but people usually do not."[32] But such a lesson is difficult to integrate at the terminal that typically delivers on its promise that we can satisfy so many desires 'in the palm of the hand,' with an 'instant download,' with 'instant access,' and 'on demand.' Summarizing his research about cell phone use among French cadres, Jauréguiberry wonders "if this new ability to connect with someone else without delay does not encourage in some cases a sort of infantile regression...."[33] For sociologist Dufour, this form of interactivity qualifies as *Sadean isolism*—an "extremist pairing of egoism and hedonism."[34] Concluding her research on cell phone use among American youth, Turkle also warns about "a real risk that we come to see others as objects to be accessed—and only for the parts we find useful, comforting, or amusing."[35] To wit, Fox and Rooney report that various features of social networking sites might be particularly conducive for individuals scoring high on 'Dark Triad' traits to achieve their objectives.[36]

Unfortunately, if the terminal is becoming increasingly personalized and responsive, face-to-face interactions are becoming decreasingly civil.[37] And in contrast to the cornucopia of options we can select to personalize our terminal experience, those individuals we meet in face-to-face encounters typically neither instantly adjust to our moods nor anticipate our constantly changing preferences. Commuting across those very different subjective experiences will require skills such as intuition, perceptiveness, patience, role-taking, empathy, and sensitivity to context. But those are categorically not the sorts of skill that one develops in terminal interactions. On the contrary, Balbus notes that such interactions "facilitate the three fundamental fantasies of the narcissism of the grandiose self: the fantasy of total control, the fantasy of perfect recognition, and the fantasy of immortality."[38]

Option unavailable

In its design, content, and functioning, the terminal provides us with an unusually intense personalized experience. In design, it promotes self-centeredness by inviting us to customize the terminal look and to materialize our unique personality in it. In so doing, we become omnipotent creators whose preferences define our terminal environment. This ability to personalize the terminal by projecting one's identity in it strengthens the sense of attachment we develop toward it. Yet, this attachment is perhaps less toward the terminal-as-object as toward the terminal-as-*experience*—the ability to connect, to immerse ourselves in the mental theme park we have created, and to access it whenever, from wherever, and on whatever device we choose. As Andrejevic points out, "if the appeal of the PC world was that of accessing the world from the privacy of home, that of pervasive interactivity ... is of being at home wherever one happens to be."[39] Empowering and comforting, this first level of personalization pertains mostly to the *surface* of the terminal.

Our terminal experience is also personalized in terms of *content*. Programmed by increasingly complex algorithms, the terminal calibrates our exposure to certain types of information, and that information typically validates our existing beliefs and attitudes. By minimizing the likelihood that we will encounter contradictory or challenging information, the terminal reduces our awareness of narratives, ideas, tastes, perceptions of reality, etc. that are radically different from our own. Seldom challenged by such alternatives, we naturally come to believe that our perceptions are indeed important, validated, and sufficient. "The shared experience of the way the physical world responds to our manipulative actions on it remains an important source of intersubjectivity," writes Franks.[40] However the personalized terminal provides us a near-perfect customized environment where the only form of intersubjectivity that matters is whatever validates the self. Similarly, urbanist Adam Greenfield argues that the personalized maps Google presents users

> erode an experience of the world in common. We can no longer even pretend that what we see on the screen is a shared, consistent representation of the same, relatively stable underlying reality. A map that interpellates us in this way ensures, in a strikingly literal sense, that we can only ever occupy and move through our own separate lifeworlds.[41]

In its functioning also, the terminal promotes the experience of personalization by gratifying our impulses, desires, interests, and fantasies on demand, and like nobody else does or can. In so doing, it tacitly normalize the terminal self's infantile impulsivity, fantasies of omnipotence, and sense of entitlement.

The other, and decidedly less 'fun,' side of personalization is the escalating delegation of work that we must now perform at the terminal. Whether we own a terminal or not, we are increasingly ordered to both educate ourselves—often individually and alone—about a constantly growing array of products, trends, services, regulations, and risks, and to use that information wisely when making important decisions about our lives. As Andrejevic put it, "we have become intelligence analysts sorting through more data than we can absorb, with ... what are proving to be inadequate resources for adjudicating amongst the diverse arrays of narratives."[42] For example, the Health Maintenance Organization I belong to suffers from a chronic turn-around rate whereby primary care physicians disappear from the 'network' faster than I really get to know them. As I find myself having to choose substitutes, it has now become my responsibility to—repeatedly—access a terminal, read information about the constantly changing pool of available doctors in 'the network,' and select one. Of course, although the information I consult in order to make such an important decision is ludicrously incomplete, I still need to 'select one option,' and *I* will have to face the consequences if the doctor I select ends up being unacceptably negligent or persistently unavailable. In other situations, we have to spend long periods of time and energy entering, formatting, and updating information at the terminals of the many organizations that make up our experience of everyday life. As those organizations "just got a new software," and as their "systems are down," it is increasingly becoming our personalized duty to accommodate to the terminals' accidents, quirks, and flawed designs. The hi-tech personalized fun we enjoy at the terminal and the falsely implied freedom it promises are but a thin veneer coating over the much more disempowering personalization of risk and exploited labor.

Notes

1 Turkle (2015).
2 Lipovetsky (2006), 39.
3 Lipovetsky (2006), 38.
4 Ebert (2011), 139.
5 Lipovetsky (2006), 14–19.
6 Roberts (2014), 3.
7 Lipovetsky (2006), 44.
8 Lipovetsky (1983), 11.
9 Castel (2005), 120.
10 Pariser (2012), 12 and 125.
11 Pariser (2012), 112.
12 Roberts (2014), 129.
13 Tisseron (2008), 224–225.
14 Bauman (2005), 87.
15 Turkle (2011).
16 Roberts (2014), 121.
17 Pariser (2012), 161.
18 Lipovetsky (1983), 16.
19 See also Heritage and Greatbatch (1986).
20 Andrejevic (2007), 193.
21 Bennett (2015), 374.
22 Roberts (2014).
23 Obama, Barack H. 2017. Farewell address. January 10.
24 Donnath (2017), 11.
25 Roberts (2014), 19.
26 Eriksen (2001).
27 Bauman (2007), 44.
28 Zimbardo and Coulombe (2015).
29 Lipovetsky (2006), 102.
30 Turkle (2011).
31 Jauréguiberry (2003).
32 Bugeja (2005), 24.
33 Jauréguiberry (2003).
34 Dufour (2008); quoted in Vande Bergh (2013), 87.
35 Turkle (2011), 154–155.
36 Fox and Rooney (2015), 163. The 'Dark Triad' is a cluster of personality traits that express narcissism, psychopathy, and Machiavellianism.
37 Bauman (2000).
38 Balbus (2005), 117.
39 Andrejevic (2007), 124.
40 Franks (2003), 625.
41 Greenfield (2017).
42 Andrejevic (2013), 3.

References

Andrejevic, Mark. 2007. *iSpy: Surveillance and Power in the Interactive Era*. Lawrence, KS: University Press of Kansas.

Andrejevic, Mark. 2013. *Infoglut: How Too Much Information Is Changing the Way We Think and Know*. New York: Routledge.

Balbus, Isaac D. 2005. *Mourning and Identity: Essays in the Psychoanalysis of Contemporary Society*. New York: Otherness.

Bauman, Zygmunt. 2000. *Liquid Modernity*. Cambridge, UK: Polity.

Bauman, Zygmunt. 2005. *Liquid Life*. Cambridge, UK: Polity.

Bauman, Zygmunt. 2007. *Consuming Life*. Cambridge, UK: Polity.

Bennett, Colin. 2015. "Trends in Voter Surveillance in Western Societies: Privacy Intrusion and Democratic Implications." *Surveillance & Society* 13(3): 370–384.

Bugeja, Michael. 2005. *Interpersonal Divide: The Search for Community in a Technological Age*. New York: Oxford University Press.

Castel, Robert. 2005. "La Face Cachée de l'individu Hypermoderne: L'individu par Défaut." pp. 119–128 in N. Aubert (ed.). *L'Individu Hypermoderne*. Toulouse: Erès.

Donnath, Judith. 2017. "The Robot Dog Fetches for Whom?" https://medium.com/berkman- klein-center/the-robot-dog-fetches-for-whom-a9c1dd0a458a. Retrieved June 15, 2017.

Dufour, Robert-Danny. 2008. *The Art of Shrinking Heads: On the New Servitude of the Liberated in the Age of Total Capitalism*. Cambridge, UK: Polity Press.

Ebert, John David. 2011. *The New Media Invasion: Digital Technologies and the World They Unmake*. Jefferson, NC: McFarlane.

Eriksen, Thomas Hylland. 2001. *The Tranny of the Moment: Fast and Slow Time in the Information Age*. London: Pluto Press.

Fox, Jesse and Margaret C. Rooney. 2015. "The Dark Triad and Trait Self-objectifications as Predictors of Men's Use and Self-Presentation Behaviors on Social Networking Sites." *Personality and Individual Differences* 76: 161–165.

Franks, David. 2003. "Mutual Interests, Different Lenses: Current Neuroscience and Symbolic Interaction." *Symbolic Interaction* 26(4): 613–630.

Greenfield, Adam. 2017. *Radical Technologies: The Design of Everyday Life*. Verso. Available at: https://longreads.com/2017/06/13/a-sociology-of-the-smartphone/. Retrieved June 14, 2017.

Heritage, John and David Greatbatch. 1986. "Generating Applause: A Study of Rhetoric and Response at Party Political Conferences." *American Journal of Sociology* 92(1): 110–157.

Jauréguiberry, Francis. 2003a. *Les Branchés du Portable*. Paris: Presse Universitaire Française.

Lipovetsky, Gilles. 1983. *L' Ère du Vide: Essais sur L'individualisme Contemporain*. Paris: Gallimard.

Lipovetsky, Gilles. 2006. *Le Bonheur Paradoxal: Essai sur la Société d'Hyperconsommation*. Paris: Gallimard.

Obama, Barack H. 2017. Farewell address. January 10.

Pariser, Eli. 2012. *The Filter Bubble: How the New Personalized Web Is Changing What We Read and How We Think*. New York: Penguin.

Roberts, Paul. 2014. *The Impulse Society: America in the Age of Instant Gratification*. New York: Bloomsbery.

Tisseron, Serge. 2008. *Virtuel, Mon Amour: Penser, Aimer, Souffrir à l'Ère des Nouvelles Technologies*. Paris: Albin Michel.

Turkle, Sherry. 2011. *Alone Together: Why We Demand More of Technology and Less of Each Other*. New York: Basic Books.

Turkle, Sherry. 2015. *Reclaiming Conversation: The Power of Talk in the Digital Age*. New York: Penguin.

Zimbardo, Phillip and Nikita D. Coulombe. 2015. *Man (Dis)connected: How Technology Has Sabotaged What It Means To Be Male*. London: Rider.

5   Validate

A third terminal default setting is that it both enables and requires users to be visible. Often explicitly dictated as a requirement of the hypermodern work-place, this imperative to visibility is central to one's sense of membership in social networks, to one's social life, and therefore, to one's sense of self. Whether by e-mails, texts, selfies, tweets, posts on social sites, or even simple clicks that transmit one's reactions to information, indicating one's presence at the terminal has become *de rigueur.* While seemingly benign, this default setting encodes how the terminal self manages the essential need for social recognition.

Inspired by George Herbert Mead, John Dewey, and William James, Frankfurt School theorist Axel Honneth posits that "the constitution of human integrity is dependent on the experience of intersubjective recogni-tion."[1] Both in an individual biography and in the history of a society, social recognition unfolds in three stages. A bit like Maslow's hierarchy of needs, those three stages pertain to changing aspects in the lives of individuals and societies, as both mature and have, over time, different needs, expectations, and motivations. At the micro-individual level, social recognition pertains first to individuals' physical integrity, then to their social one, and then to their personal one. At the macro level, the major conflicts and stages of devel-opment in the history of modern society also evidence parallel successive stages. Those consist of: the struggles over social-economic rights (physical integrity), over political-legal rights (social integrity), and over personal rights (individual integrity).

Individuals who are granted recognition of their *physical* integrity are treated—typically in the family—with the love, care, and freedom necessary to develop as individuals. As a result they feel free to act, autonomous, and develop self-confidence. Physical violence, abuse, rape, torture, imprison-ment, and other forms of corporeal degradation violate a person's physical integrity. In addition to concrete physical injuries, people who suffer this condition experience a loss of trust, autonomy, and self-confidence. Many nineteenth and twentieth revolutions and workers' movements are good examples of social conflicts pertaining to the recognition of physical integrity. Participants demanded basic inalienable rights as human beings, and freedom from the coercive powers of the monarchy, fascism, slavery, capitalism, and other systems they deemed oppressive. Concretely, they demanded to be protected from the physical violence they routinely and systemically experienced in the forms of starvation, death, dangerous working conditions, slavery, torture, imprisonment, etc. This type of social recognition was formalized in declarations of human rights, labor laws, and in anti-poverty, health, housing, education, and other policies.

Individuals who are granted recognition of their *social* integrity are treated with respect, fairness, equality, and inclusion. As a result, they develop self-respect. When individuals' social integrity is challenged, discredited, or denied, they experience shame and a loss of self-respect. The 1960s Civil Rights movement is a good example of this second type of recognition. Participants demanded equality under the law and acknowledgment as "morally and cognitively accountable citizens."[2] Concretely, they wanted to be treated equally and fairly, and to be protected from the social-legal violence they routinely and systemically experienced in the forms of discrimination, inequality, social exclusion, and ostracism. Of course, this does not mean that in the 1960s, Black Americans had won recognition of their physical integrity. On the contrary, in many regions of the US, violence against them was routine and rarely punished, especially when the perpetrator was white.[3] And the history of the Civil Rights movement is replete with vicious beatings, firebombs, and cold-blooded murder. The contemporary slogan "Black Lives Matter" suggests that this disregard for the physical integrity of Black Americans remains an explosive issue. However, the drive of the Civil Rights movement concerned the recognition of social and political rights. This form of recognition was formalized in the Civil Rights Act and anti-discrimination laws.

Individuals granted recognition of their *personal* integrity are treated with acceptance, support, and validation. Being valued for who they are, they experience self-esteem. When they are denigrated, dismissed, ridiculed, considered deficient or inferior, they experience a loss of self-esteem. The LGBQT movement struggle is a good example of this third type of recognition. Participants demand not just the right to feel physically safe (first form of recognition), and to have equal rights under the law (second form), they also demand equal social acceptance. Concretely, they want to be treated with the same spirit of inclusion, support, consideration, and esteem as everyone else, and be protected from the social psychological violence they routinely experience in the forms of individual degradation. This form of recognition has been formalized in various legislations, the establishment of LGBQT community centers, civil organizations, businesses, academic and multicultural education programs, for example.

Struggles for the recognition of physical integrity concern economic issues, struggles for the recognition of social integrity concern political-legal ones, and struggles for the recognition of personal integrity concern social psychological ones. In other words, they entail *interaction*. Except in cases of psychological troubles, our self-esteem depends on how others respond to our self-performance, and how we imagine their responses. Ultimately, these responses consist of interactions. And while we rarely interpret how others respond to our self-performance with complete accuracy, we can typically distinguish between those gestures that convey inclusion, acceptance, respect, support, and esteem, those that fail to do so, and those that purposefully convey their opposites. As Daniel Goleman documents, we attend to those gestures at the neural level.[4] However, as I develop below, just as the need for personal recognition has become especially salient in the hypermodern moment, the "visibility" default setting at the terminal complicates the satisfaction of this need in significantly new ways.

Click here to enlarge

"Stay Extraordinary," touts a *Coca Cola* ad. "This is the story of *you*, the *incredible you*," cheers a female voice-over on the commercial ad selling *23andMe*—the software that will guide customers through joyful genetic self-discovery. Hypermodern theorists suggest that in contemporary society, it is no longer sufficient to be reasonably well educated, to have a reasonably comfortable life, and to be reasonably successful in one's professional and domestic endeavors. One must also be (or at least, project the image of being) healthy, attractive, interesting, happy, centered, flexible, entertaining, cool, well-adjusted, informed, creative, spiritual, socially intelligent, and responsibly libidinous.[5] As De Gaulejac puts it, contemporary individuals

> must be similar yet different, affiliated yet unaffiliated, common and uncommon, ordinary and extraordinary ... We define ourselves less by our similarities to others than through exception, as if to be like everybody else was to be hopelessly *any*body ... We must thus escape the ordinary, reach beyond ourselves, evade common categories, and project ourselves in the conquest of the grandiose self.[6]

While individuals denied social recognition experience rejection as well as a host of other adverse emotional, social, and physiological consequences,[7] in hypermodern society, the traditional mechanisms individuals use to manage this need have all but disappeared, and the criteria they use to obtain or bestow it are rapidly changing. In such conditions, hypermodern individuals quite understandably struggle with the nagging anxiety of "being just themselves"[8] and others succumb to a new form of depression, which sociologist Alain Ehrenberg diagnoses as "la fatigue d'être soi" (the tiredness of being oneself).[9] For sociologist van den Bergh also, this new form of depression emerges in a culture where "incitement has replaced prohibition as a main motivator of behavior." As he explains,

> what is expected from the individual is not restriction and sublimation but mobilization and expression of his passions. Henceforth the thing is

to get the most out of oneself. One needs to be oneself and become it even more … Human despondency thus is no longer understood in terms of conflict and guilt, but of defect and shame … Depression in this context appears as failure in what is being called for. Being depressed means not being able or willing to have a project, be enterprising, assertive, on the move. It means being unwilling or unable to realize oneself.[10]

For Hartmut Rosa, this depressed tiredness is not just caused by an abstract existential angst, but by the objective conditions of everyday life:

contemporary society … produces guilty subjects who can hope for neither remission nor forgiveness. We must pay the price for all our deficiencies and failures, and the growing mass of all those who—because of unemployment—are excluded from the hamster's wheel reminds us how expensive that price is.[11]

As he notes, while in previous eras individual recognition was bestowed post-factum, to crown a successful life, the type of social recognition contemporary individuals seek—or must resign themselves to—no longer celebrates a life-long achievement or status. Rather, it rewards *performance*. It has become a daily struggle whose rules are constantly ratcheted up, and waged with the reasonably fatalistic understanding that our accomplishments can be neither accumulated nor guaranteed currency in the unstable future.[12] On the contrary, writes Rosa, any acquired skill, possession, or competency that is not regularly updated quickly "sinks into anachronism": "Whoever does not constantly adapt to those conditions of constant change (or does not permanently update hardwares and softwares—in the real and metaphorical sense) foregoes all possibilities of remaining connected to his/her era and to confront the future."[13] For Zawadzki, the problem of social recognition in contemporary society is a central crisis of our institutions and the verdict of their failure. With all their pseudo-rites, merits, awards, mass-printed 'certificates of excellence,' and other digitized tokens rewarding performance, contemporary institutions not only fail to genuinely satisfy the need for recognition, they corrupt its meaning and intensify the sense of loss for its absence.[14]

Historically, granting esteem entailed face-to-face interaction with known members of relatively stable communities, who would convey this status through physical gestures, sensory rituals, sacred objects bestowed in public ceremonies, announcements, etc. Lacking those, confronting both 'communication malaise'[15] and the 'anxiety of hyperchoice,'[16] hypermodern individuals turn to terminal interactions in the hopes of fulfilling the need for social recognition, a need which is now reduced to constant and facile visibility. As De Gaulejac puts it "to see and to be seen seem to be the only criteria that give some sort of meaning to an ephemeral existence."[17]

Share

"Express Yourself," "Broadcast Yourself," "Upload Yourself," "Be Heard," "Be Visible," "Be Yourself," "Be Different."[18] As an increasingly important space for self-presentation and social recognition, the 'tyrannical' default setting of visibility demands "a continuous and unlimited production of the self," write Aubert and Haroche.[19] For example, users of social networking sites find it necessary to constantly upgrade their online self-presentation and to keep everyone informed about their evolving interests, hobbies, changes of address, accomplishments, relationship status, insights, or memberships in the constantly growing number of communities or associations (online or otherwise) to which they belong. Although exhausting and stressful, users keep coming back because so much of social life unfolds in terminal interactions, on social networking sites.[20] As Rainier and Wellman emphasize, "people are not hooked on gadgets; they are hooked to each other."[21] For Roberts, "to be seen by others is increasingly regarded as a requirement for personal and social advance. We are successful to the degree that our self-expression is consumed by others."[22] For Baudrillard also, "nothing is true unless it is desecrated, objectified, stripped of its aura, or dragged onstage."[23] And as Barus-Michel notes,

> one must sustain the other's attention, or his gaze. There cannot be any dead moment, negativity, risk of falling into the hole, of being forgotten. One must continue, the spectacle must go on. The content of the message is not important, it is the spectacle that matters, not the listening.[24]

However, the fun experience of omnipresence and cathartic spontaneity at the terminal is also motivated by the constant fear of being demoted to what Bauman calls the *precariat*: being invisible, ignored, found unworthy of empathy, recognition, or consideration.[25] As Aubert and Haroche point out, when we mistake the invisible for the insignificant or non-existent, this visibility:

> satisfies a demand—imagined or real—for legitimacy and beyond that, and more fundamentally, for recognition. The individual is therefore considered, appreciated, and judged through the quantity of signs, of texts, and of images that he produces, and which he is induced to constantly produce.[26]

For Turkle also, "connectivity becomes a craving. When we receive a text or an email, our nervous system responds by giving us a shot of dopamine. We are stimulated by connectivity itself. We learn to require it, even as it depletes us."[27] Tellingly, one of the most infamous worms that infected tens of millions of computers on May 6, 2000 was activated by clicking—in a mass-distributed e-mail—on a link titled "ILOVEYOU." Apparently, few could resist.

The famous Time/Life picture of president Lyndon Johnson exposing his physical scar to the nation has been replaced by the terminal-as-therapeutic-space, where every user is invited to 'share' psychological and social scars to a scattered and invisible audience.[28] At the terminal self-realization is confused with self-absorption,[29] and the Delphic oracle's injunction to know oneself becomes the compulsion to show oneself.[30]

Structured by digital codes and exploiting deep anxieties, this imperative to visibility "reduces individuals solely to their appearances, frequently inhibits the possibility of critical thought, flattens the separation between the imaginary and the mode of existence, and impoverishes everyone's internal space," write Nicole Aubert.[31]

And since intimacy is notoriously difficult to achieve at the terminal,[32] users can still gratify what Serge Tisseron calls 'extimacy'—"showing certain aspects of our intimate self, so that others can validate them and, in so doing, increase those aspects' values in our own minds."[33] Feeling compelled to disclose increasingly private intimate parts of themselves at the terminal and to maximize the number of clicks they receive, the terminal self may feel compelled to post statements that become progressively more self-damaging.[34] For Spurk, also this imperative increasingly robs us of our creativity:

> We experience it as a type of obligation to expose one's intimacy on the public space, and—as a form of self-inflicted violence—to give oneself to the other's gaze and judgment: a visibility that makes me more vulnerable and defenseless by removing everything that is particular and specific to my being.[35]

This enforced intimacy, this enforced collapse of all distance between one's inner feelings and virtually anyone destroys the distance necessary for *respect*. It celebrates a pornography of the soul and the psyche, which is all the more tragic since no one is really interested, except perhaps the psychological voyeur.

The sheer dynamics of those recognition-seeking transmissions that daily circulate, bounce off each other, amplify, become viral, and disappear are mind-boggling. And so is the number of those messages, their velocities, and intensities. Since one shortcut to get recognition is to reveal increasingly private and personal aspects of oneself, and since one's audience is frazzled and distracted by competing calls for immediate attention, excess becomes the operating principle. I exaggerate, therefore I exist. As Twitter co-founder Evan Williams also acknowledges, "the trouble with the internet … is that it rewards extremes."[36] In a number of other infamous cases, individuals inflict bizarre violence on self and others for the purpose of instant celebrity on social media sites.[37] And as recent political events in the U.S., Europe, and elsewhere suggest, this new intensity in self-presentation can be charged negatively, amplified, channeled outward, and targeted.

Auto-correct

Curiously, all the promises of freedom to express one's unique self at the terminal have failed to produce the proverbial 'blooming of 10,000 flowers.' Or perhaps, they wilted as soon as they became digitized. For example, Facebook users tend to present a self that is constricted by a narrow range of options, that is flattened to the 'lowest common denominator,' and that is assembled so as not to offend anyone in the network, or even a future audience.[38] Highly sensitive to others' judgments, the terminal self has much less texture, nuance, and complexity than the person typing it at the keyboard. Calling them 'hyper-other-directed,' Turkle reports that teenagers who use social media tend to need others to validate their thoughts and emotions in order to experience them as real.[39] At the group level, Hampton et al. find that social media users contribute to a 'spiral of silence' and members are unlikely to voice unpopular political opinions. Those researchers also worry that this spiral of silence at the terminal might replicate in face-to-face interaction. As they warn, "the broad awareness social media users have of their networks might make them more hesitant to speak up because they are especially tuned into the opinions of those around them."[40] Hence, if the terminal self seems aggressively self-promoting and wildly inflated, s/he is in fact weak and insecure,[41] hopes to feel as little as possible, lacks affect, and a sense of autonomy.[42] These dispositions are not limited to terminal interactions, and Turkle reminds us that over time, the performance of our terminal identity "may feel like identity itself."[43] Nygren and Gidlund capture this condition as "digital alienation." As they explain:

> individuals perform themselves on the stage of digital culture, and their control of the performance is lost because of the conditions of the digital performance ... We are no longer in control of the "self" we perform. We censor our thoughts and our images in relation to the expected (the life-styling logic) and the product/the self becomes alienated. We lose control of our digital selves and the world we live in, and it is hard to feel committed to the self since the analogue or localized life is separated from the digital.[44]

In addition, research conducted by Gardner and Davis[45] and Turkle[46] find that young people feel obligated to communicate only positive news about themselves, thereby implying that—like everybody else in their networks—they are living happy, exciting, successful, and carefree lives. For Rugoff,

> the underlying fantasy that we should all be ceaselessly enjoying ourselves in some hyperactive simulation of childhood adds up to a new kind of puritanism. Pleasure is no longer prohibited, but is now relentlessly imposed as an imperative. Not to be having fun amounts to an admission of social ineptitude, and the price we pay for this is a consuming and corrosive unease.[47]

As Barus-Michel also notes: "Once, people said 'to live happy, let's live hidden.' Today it's the opposite: 'Let's be visible, let's make others envy us, let's be noticed.' Narcissism is insatiable and feeds itself by the other's gaze."[48] Yet, this constant terminal exposure to 'glammed up'[49] and obsessive signs of success can have deleterious effects on readers, as they eventually come to re-evaluate their own lives as lame in comparison to the exciting adventures and cool lifestyles their friends visibly document in the endless flow of Facebook 'one-way dispatches.'[50]

While some individuals might post excessively (and obsessively) positive self-representations at the terminal because they want to provoke envy, several of my students also admit that they don't want to "bum out" their friends by communicating negative or sad news. Those might reveal one's failings while implicitly requiring members of their network to perform per-functory and artificial emotion work on their behalf.

On the other hand, if reading about others' exciting lives might prompt feelings of being lame, Facebook users who evaluate their own carefully premeditated 'profiles' experience an increase in self-esteem.[51] Hence, the self-flattering 'packaged self' that users develop and stage at the terminal becomes self-validating and prompts more of the same.[52] As a result of this distortion, terminal users might be less likely to be exposed to posts about the tragedies, struggles, and defeats that inevitably punctuate everyday life in the hypermodern moment. Having little exposure to those events, they may be less able to understand and compose with them when they do appear 'in real life.'

Scroll down

Sharing is Caring. Spread the Word.[53]

If positive posts dominate Facebook in terms of sheer number, negative ones command our attention in terms of impact. More precisely, while the reduc-tion of 'bummer' news at the terminal obscures from view and mind a signi-ficant share of human experience, *how* they appear there already alters their meanings. Since the terminal software formats how users can communicate about unfortunate events, they also necessarily structure how the audience will interpret and respond to them. Note that the very decision to use Face-book posts, e-mails, or short messages to communicate about such events to an invisible and scattered network is itself already perplexing. Regardless of motivation, however, receptors of such messages become a de facto captive but isolated audience, randomly forced into shock, outrage, sadness, or fear. I am sure that every reader has similar stories to tell, but in the past few months, I have had to attend to Facebook posts commenting on: an acrimo-nious divorce, crippling accidents, toxic relationships, distressing illnesses, a devastating suicide, brutal assaults, and ugly betrayals. In five sentences or less. In other cases, I was implicitly asked to respond to terminal communiqués whose authors were (at times) graphically depicting their hallucinations, incoherently venting their delusions, publicly degrading their former partners, reporting 'live' on panic attacks, or rambling through substance-induced delirium.[54] As Baudrillard asks,

> And mad cow disease? Are we not, as the human species, like these poor mad cows? Aren't we being made to swallow, on every level, a strange bone meal—all of these ground-up messages, all of this meal of advertising and media production, this giant, milled junk heap of the news that we are stuffed with—like the meal made of bone, corpses and carcasses that we stuff our cows with—it is all bringing our species closer to spongiform encephalopathy.[55]

In addition to the intensely negative emotions triggered by such posts, the very *context* in which they appear also transforms their impact. For example, scrolling down my Facebook newsfeed for about five minutes,

- I smile at a *Good Morning* message, then
- feel my heart stop when reading about anti-semitic attacks; then
- relax with a video-clip of a perfect sunrise, then
- laugh at a cute panda video-clip, then
- am saddened by an old friend's post indicating he's off the wagon again, then
- chuckle at a joke, then
- shiver at a friend's post announcing his son's suicide, then
- cringe at an audio-clip posted by a musician friend, then
- angrily click on the "close" tab of an irritating commercial ad pop-up, then
- jump in my chair, heart pounding, startled by the loud music suddenly blasting from the terminal speakers, then
- grin, as I am musing on a Zen koan, then
- feel queasy at images of decapitated human heads nonchalantly tossed around by ISIS psychopaths, then
- dive into the video-clip of a euphoric ocean, then
- wonder about an announcement for a sociological conference, then
- giggle at another joke.

When messages prompting intensely negative emotions randomly interrupt any other message, the terminal self's experience can rapidly oscillate between a smile and a frown, delight and nausea, dopamine and adrenaline. What are the short and long-term neural effects of this type of interactivity on the terminal self's emotional temper and how does it shape one's ability to respond effectively, ethically, and empathically to adverse situations?

Selfies

If everyday life in contemporary social institutions often reduces users to algorithms, terminal interactions validate each user's unique identity and predilections. As flattering mirrors and echo chambers, they provide a semblance of social recognition in the age of isolation and disrespect.[56] In order to enjoy such comforts, however, users must submit to software codes that significantly constrain how they can represent themselves and interact with others at the terminal. Performing under such conditions, the terminal self becomes a 'selfie'—a distorted digital impression of the person typing at the keyboard. It is a premeditated self-presentation that users have purposefully formatted for acceptance and recognition *light*. They do so by trading the right of privacy for the pleasure of constant visibility; originality for acceptability; the engaged and sustained exchange for the facile and faceless "likes." As the criteria enabling one to reap such pseudo-signs of recognition are constantly changing and require increasingly deep layers of intimacy, the user's experience of recognition and self-concept significantly alters. This change is not restricted to the terminal self's online subjective experience, but, as I develop in the next chapter, disrupts face-to-face interactions and relations.

Notes

1 Honneth (1992), 189.
2 Honneth (1992).
3 U.S. Civil Rights Congress (1970).
4 Goleman (2006).
5 Aubert (2005a and 2005b).
6 De Gaulejac (2005), 132.
7 Honneth (1995).
8 De Gaulejac (2005), 132.
9 Ehrenberg (2000).
10 Van den Bergh (2013), 92.
11 Rosa (2012), 81.
12 Ibid.
13 Rosa (2010), 148.
14 Zawadzki (2011), 294.
15 Aubert (2005a).
16 Ascher (2012).
17 De Gaulejac (2011), 256.
18 All those are commercial ads for internet-related services.
19 Aubert and Haroche (2011), 7.
20 Gottschalk and Whitmer (2013), 10.
21 Rainie and Wellman (2012), 3.
22 Roberts (2014), 136.
23 Baudrillard (2010), 67.
24 Barus-Michel (2011), 31.
25 Bauman and Donskis (2013).
26 Aubert and Haroche (2011), 8.
27 Turkle (2011), 225.

28 Turkle (2011).
29 Roberts (2014), 138.
30 Rosen (2007), 16.
31 Aubert and Haroche (2011), 8.
32 Gardner and Davis (2013).
33 Tisseron (2011a).
34 Tisseron (2011b).
35 Spurk (2011), 324.
36 Streitfeld (2017).
37 Mariani (2016); see also Coll (2017).
38 Marwick and boyd (2010).40
39 Turkle (2011).
40 Hampton et al. (2014).
41 Roberts (2014), 133.
42 Gardner and Davis (2013), 78 and 85.
43 Turkle (2011), 12.
44 Nygren and Gidlund (2016), 406.
45 Gardner and Davis (2013).
46 Turkle (2011).
47 Rugoff (1995), 147.
48 Barus-Michel (2011), 31.
49 Gardner and Davis (2013), 64.
50 Gardner and Davis (2013), 109; see also Winter (2013).
51 Gonzales and Hancock (2011).
52 Gardner and Davis (2013), 61; see also Van Koningsbruggen et al. (2017), 334.
53 Facebook ad.
54 Often prescription drugs.
55 Baudrillard (2010), 99.
56 Honneth (2007).

References

Ascher, Francois. 2012. "La Société Hypermoderne." *Société Digitale*. www.culture-mobile.net/quotidien-intelligent/individu-hypermoderne.

Aubert, Nicole and Claudine Haroche. 2011 "Être Visible pour Exister: L'Injonction à la Visibilité." pp. 7–22 in *Les Tyrannies de la Visibilité: Être Visible Pour Exister?*, Nicole Aubert and Claudine Haroche (eds.). Toulouse: Érès.

Aubert, Nicole. 2005a. "Un Individu Paradoxal." pp. 13–24 in *L'Individu Hypermoderne*, Nicole Aubert (ed.). Toulouse: Érès.

Aubert, Nicole. 2005b. "L'Intensité de Soi." pp. 73–87 in *L'Individu Hypermoderne*, Nicole Aubert (ed.). Toulouse: Érès.

Barus-Michel, Jacqueline. 2011. "Une Société sur Écrans." pp. 25–52 in *Les Tyrannies de la Visibilité: Être Visible Pour Exister?*, Nicole Aubert and Claudine Haroche (eds.). Toulouse: Érès

Baudrillard, Jean. 2010. *The Agony of Power*. Cambridge, MA: MIT Press (Semiotext(e)).

Bauman, Zygmunt and Leonidas Donskis. 2013. *Moral Blindness: The Loss of Sensibility in Liquid Modernity*. Cambridge, UK: Polity.

Coll, Steve. 2017. "Facebook and the Murderer" *New York Times* April 16. www.newyorker.com/news/daily-comment/facebook-and-the-murderer?mbid=nl_170418_Daily&CNDID=49051958&spMailingID=10846255&spUserID=MTgyNjU5NDYyNjA4S0&spJobID=1141426585&spReportId=MTE0MTQyNjU4NQS2.

De Gaulejac, Vincent. 2005. "Le Sujet Manqué: L'Individu face aux Contradictions de l'Hypermodernité." pp. 129–143 in *L'Individu Hypermoderne*, Nicole Aubert (ed.). Toulouse: Érès.

De Gaulejac, Vincent. 2011. "Entre Dissimulation et ostentation: Le Traitement de l'Envie dans les Sociétés contemporaines." pp. 245–257 in *Les Tyrannies de la Visibilité: Être Visible Pour Exister?*, Nicole Aubert and Claudine Haroche (eds.). Toulouse: Erès.

Ehrenberg, Alain. 2000. *La Fatigue D'Être Soi*. Paris: Odile Jacob.

Gardner, Howard and Katie Davis. 2013. *The App Generation: How Today's Youth Navigate Identity, Intimacy, and Imagination in a Digital World*. New Haven, CT: Yale University Press.

Goleman, Daniel. 2006. *Social Intelligence: Beyond IQ, Beyond Emotional Intelligence*. New York: Bantam.

Gonzales, Amy L. and Jeffrey T. Hancock. 2011. "Mirror, Mirror on my Facebook Wall: Effects of Exposure to Facebook on Self-Esteem." *Cyberpsychology, Behavior, and Social Networking* 14(1–2): 79–83.

Gottschalk, Simon and Jennifer Whitmer. 2013. "Hypermodern Dramaturgy in Online Encounters." pp. 309–334 in *The Drama of Social Life: A Dramaturgical Handbook*, Charles Edgley (ed.). Ashgate.

Hampton, K. N., L. Rainie, W. Lu, M. Dwyer, I. Shin, and K. Purcell. 2014. "Social Media and the Spiral of Silence." Washington D.C.: Pew Research Center.

Honneth, Axel. 1992. "Integrity and Disrespect: Principles of a Conception of Morality Based on the Theory of Recognition." *Political Theory* 29(2): 187–201.

Honneth, Axel. 1995. *The Struggle for Recognition: The Moral Grammar of Social Conflicts*. Cambridge, UK: Polity Press.

Honneth, Axel. 2007. *Disrespect: The Normative Foundations of Critical Theory*. Cambridge, UK: Polity.

Mariani, Mike. 2016. "The Antisocial Network." *Psychology Today* 49(5): 80–88.

Marwick, Alice and danah boyd. 2010. "I Tweet Honestly, I Tweet Passionately: Twitter Users, Context Collapse, and the Imagined Audience." *New Media & Society* 13(1): 114–133.

Nygren, Katarina Giritli and Katarina L. Gidlund. 2016. "The Pastoral Power of Technology: Rethinking Alienation in Digital Culture." pp. 398–412 in *Marx in the Age of Digital Capitalism*, Christian Fuchs and Vincent Mosco (eds.). Leiden: Brill.

Pariser, Eli. 2011. *The Filter Bubble: How the New Personalized Web is Changing What We Read and How We Think*. New York: Penguin.

Rainie, Lee and Barry Wellman. 2012. *Networked: The New Social Operating System*. Cambridge, MA: MIT Press.

Roberts, Paul. 2014. *The Impulse Society: America in the Age of Instant Gratification*. New York: Bloomsbury.

Rosa, Hartmut. 2010. *Accélération: Une Critique Sociale du Temps*. Paris: La Découverte.

Rosa, Hartmut. 2012. *Aliénation et Accélération: Vers une Théorie Critique de la Modernité Tardive*. Paris: La Découverte.

Rosen, Christine. 2007. "Virtual Friendship and the New Narcissism." *The New Atlantis*. Summer.

Rugoff, Ralph. 1995. *Circus Americanus*. London: Verso.

Spurk, Jan. 2011. "De La Reconaissance á l'Insignificance." pp. 323–333 in *Les Tyrannies de la Visibilité: Être Visible Pour Exister?*, Nicole Aubert and Claudine Haroche (eds.). Toulouse: Érès.

Streitfeld, David. 2017. "'The Internet Is Broken': @ev Is Trying to Salvage It." *New York Times.* May 21, 2017. www.nytimes.com/2017/05/20/technology/evan-williams-medium-twitter-internet.html.

Tisseron, Serge. 2011a. "Les Nouveaux Réseaux Sociaux: Visibilité et Invisibilité sur le Net." pp. 119–130 in *Les Tyrannies de la Visibilité: Être Visible Pour Exister?* Nicole Aubert and Claudine Haroche (eds.). Toulouse: Erès.

Tisseron, Serge. 2011b. "Intimité et Extimité." *Communications* 1(88): 83–91.

Turkle, Sherry. 2011. *Alone Together: Why We Demand More of Technology and Less of Each Other.* New York: Basic Books.

U.S. Civil Rights Congress. 1970. *We Charge Genocide: The Historic Petition to the United Nations for Relief from a Crime of the United States Government against the Negro people.* New York: International Publishers.

Van den Bergh, Bert. 2013. "Depression: Resisting Ultra-Liberalism?" pp. 81–102 in *The Social Pathologies of Contemporary Civilization,* Kieran Keohane and Anders Petersen (eds.). Farnham, UK: Ashgate.

Van Koningsbruggen, Guido M., Tilo Hartmann, Allison Eden, and Harm Veling. 2017. "Spontaneous Hedonic Reactions to Social Media Cues." *Cyberpsychology, Behavior, and Social Networking* 20(5): 334–340.

Winter, Stephan, Caroline Brückner, and Nicole Krämer. 2015. "They Came, They Liked, They Commented: Social Influence on Facebook News Channels." *Cyberpsychology, Behavior, and Social Networking* 18(8): 431–436.

Zawadzki, Paul. 2011. "Le Regard Vertical." pp. 293–302 in *Les Tyrannies de la Visibilité: Être Visible Pour Exister?,* Nicole Aubert and Claudine Haroche (eds.). Toulouse: Erès.

6 Ignore[1]

"Jimmy, I do not care for your condescending tone. Your duties as my graduate assistant are now finished." Pr. Stanley's e-mail shot right through Jimmy's heart, making him feel queasy. Panicked, he forwards me the e-mail, and as graduate coordinator, I have to urgently go on 'damage control' mode. Analyzing these e-mail exchanges, trying to locate the fateful sentence that triggered this crisis, I am reminded of other similar incidents I've had to manage. Because I am interested in e-mail communication, students, colleagues, and friends often drop by my office to share stories of pain, outrage, and panic they experienced at the terminal. Everyone has a story. By the time Pr. Stanley's answer slammed on Jimmy's terminal screen, it was too late. I had to reassign Jimmy to work with another instructor, and I don't think he and Pr. Stanley ever spoke again. So, while many scholars are busy quantifying the precise numbers of hostile e-mails circulating between people in various organizations, Jimmy's story reminds us that just one bad e-mail can ruin a relation.

The e-mail crisis between Pr. Stanley and Jimmy follows the now familiar sequence of the 'emotional hit-and-run.' It entails two or more individuals interacting at the terminal through short e-mail messages, and then:

- a sentence whose 'tone' a recipient misinterprets as offensive, dismissive, sarcastic, or disrespectful;
- the recipient's response, in the form of a short digital burst of anger whose intensity seems inappropriate; and
- aggressive silence.

As I hope will become clear below, this silence is significant and the incident does not end with the silence. The social, psychological, and neural scars of the verbal (and often public) duel become part of the protagonists' biography: they can re-appear in and distort face-to-face interaction. When other individuals witness the incident, they too can be affected by it, both directly and indirectly; both immediately and later.

"All communication, even the most trivial, has the power to do one of three things: maintain the status quo; bring people closer together; or drive them further apart," write Shipley and Schwalbe.[2] Unsurprisingly, one of the two main reasons we use the terminal is connectivity—our ability to communicate with others. In 2011, cell phone users worldwide exchanged over two trillion text messages, and in June 2017, Facebook claimed 1.74 billion users. If Facebook were a country, it would be the third largest in the world. As Pariser notes,

> 900,000 blogs, 50 million tweets, more than 60 million Facebook updates, and 210 billion e-mails are sent off in into the electronic ether every day. Eric Schmidt [Google CEO] likes to point out that if you recorded all human communication from the dawn of time to 2003, it'd take up about 5 billion gigabytes of storage space. Now we're creating that much data in two *days*.[3]

However, as we use our terminal mainly for *connectivity*—the fourth default setting—it significantly shapes how we do so, both at the terminal and in face-to-face interaction.

Face-work

For Goffman, our everyday life is punctuated by encounters where we act out a 'line'—a pattern of verbal and nonverbal acts by which we express how we view the situation, how we view those we encounter, and how we view ourselves. To act out a line, we present a 'face,' which Goffman defines as the "positive social value we effectively claim for ourselves during a particular encounter." In other words, when I interact with you, I behave in ways that indicate to you that I am a certain kind of person, who finds himself in a particular context, that is populated by specific others. Implicit in everyday encounters is the expectation that you will accept the face I present and will support the line I am performing. This expectation is of course mutual. In an encounter, we perform *defensive* gestures that help us sustain the face we present ('pride'), and *protective* gestures that support the faces the others present ('considerateness'). We are tacitly expected to "save the feelings and the face of others present" and are generally "disinclined to witness the defacement of others." As Goffman elegantly put it, "the person who can witness another's humiliation and unfeelingly retain a cool countenance himself is said to be 'heartless,' just as he who can unfeelingly participate in his own defacement is thought to be 'shameless'."[4] For Bauman also:

> In this realm of face-to-face interaction, individuality is asserted and daily renegotiated in the continuous activity of interaction. To be an 'individual' is to accept an alienable responsibility for the course and consequence of interaction.[5]

Pride and considerateness are intertwined. In an encounter, I must protect my own face without threatening yours, and I must protect your face without endangering mine. And as benign as those gestures might seem, Goffman considers face-work to be not just as essential *of* interaction, but as essential *to* interaction. As he notes, "maintenance of face is a *condition* of interaction, not its objective ... To study face-saving is to study the traffic rules of social interaction."[6] Through these minute adjustments, we collaborate to sustain each other's face and hence, the *expressive order*—an "order that regulates the flow of events so that they remain consistent with participants' faces." This order is important because face is not in our possession. As Goffman reminds us, it is "only on loan from society and can be withdrawn if we do not behave in a way that is worthy of it."[7]

In every social encounter, therefore, we run the risk of losing face, and when others challenge, ignore, or discredit the line we are acting, we feel "out of face," "in the wrong face" or "shamefaced." Those 'incidents'—as Goffman calls them—can be self-inflicted or inflicted by another. They can be accidental, malicious, or incidental. Above all, as the medium through which we seek esteem, grant it, deny it, or suffer its rebuff, face is "a sacred thing." The need to save face seems to be universal, and "each person, sub-culture, and society seems to have its own characteristic repertoire of face-saving practices."[8]

Face-work refers to those practices; it consists of the verbal and non-verbal gestures we perform in order to prevent face-threatening incidents, and to resolve them when they occur. There are two basic types of face-work. The *preventive* type aims at protecting participants' faces. They include familiar gestures such as: waiting to see what line one is allowed to take, presenting oneself with modesty, offering belittling claims, showing lack of seriousness, self-censoring, performing courtesies and tactful blindness, avoiding contact or risky situations, withdrawing, using go-betweens, staying off topic and away from activities that would reveal inconsistencies in the lines participants are performing.

When face-threatening incidents occur and avoidance is no longer possible, participants are expected to perform *restorative* face-work. This common ritual typically proceeds in four steps:

- Step 1: *Challenge*: When my action threatens the face you are presenting, you, other participants in the encounter, and even I may openly challenge that action.
- Step 2: *Offering*: I am expected to apologize to you.
- Step 3: *Acceptance*: You are expected to accept my apology.
- Step 4: *Thanks*: I must show gratitude that you accepted my apology.

At times, we may consciously acknowledge, reflect, and comment on those restorative gestures; at other times, they are unconscious. In many cases, they are so routine as to go unnoticed; they are "like traditional plays in a game or traditional steps in a dance."[9]

Interactions are *communicative* acts; they process information. For psychologist Howard Gardner, this processing capacity is "a biopsychological potential to process specific forms of information in certain kinds of ways. Human beings have evolved diverse information-processing capacities—I term these 'intelligences'—that allow them to solve problems or to fashion products."[10]

In face-to-face encounters, we typically communicate via nine channels: *language, paralanguage, facial expressions, kinesics, haptics, proxemics, chronemics, actions,* and *objects.* We transmit information through these channels both willingly and unknowingly, both consciously and unconsciously. Defined in this way, most social behaviors can be understood as communicative acts. We perform the self, establish our relations with others, and participate in everyday life through communicative acts. Many of our emotions, thoughts, and behaviors are responses to others' communicative acts, and we manifest them as communicative acts. Except for the physical realm, our most agonizing pains and most gratifying pleasures result from communicative acts.[11]

As an intelligent species, we "naturally" adapt our communicative acts to the *settings* where we encounter one another. We whisper to each other at the opera, but scream in each other's ears at a rock concert. We describe a scene differently in a phone conversation than in a letter. We raise our hand in the classroom and gesture 'air-writing' in a crowded diner. We sometimes make mental notes about those physical settings and mention them to others in the flow of interaction. Similarly, when we use terminal devices—when we 'go online' to interact with others—we enter a "behavior setting"[12] or a "socio-mental space" that prompts distinctive ways of interacting. As Suler puts it,

> when they power up their computers, launch a program, write e-mail, or log onto their online service, users often feel—consciously or subconsciously—that they are entering a 'place' or 'space' that is filled with a wide array of meanings and purposes.[13]

Check e-mail

From a Skype conversation, to a text message, a phone conversation, or an e-mail, the terminal provides us with various platforms to communicate with others. While each of these platforms presents distinct challenges that users must resolve in order to communicate efficiently, I will focus especially on e-mail. There are several reasons justifying this choice. One, some of the challenges to efficient communication present in e-mail also exist in other text-based platforms. Two, while young people are increasingly communicating via short text messages,[14] e-mail has already become established as a main tool of management within and across bureaucratic organizations and similar adult entities.[15] According to Purcell, 92 percent of American adults who go online own an e-mail account, and virtually every white-collar worker employed in a bureaucratic organization has one as well.[16] In a recent research, she also found that American workers cite e-mail as their most important tool,[17] and Rainie and Wellman find that "e-mail is the single online activity that draws the most users on any given day."[18] Gitlin also points out that "through the most mundane act of e-mailing ... you exist and affirm the other's existence ... Intellectuals may scoff, but it is this relatively trivial mercy that most people in consumerist culture seek much of the time."[19] Research also reveals that office workers check their in-box about 30 to 40 times a day[20] and spend an average of 23 percent of their working day managing e-mails.[21]

Unfortunately, most e-mail users do not click on their in-box with the same sort of enchanting romantic élan depicted in movies such as *You've Got Mail*, or others. On the contrary, notes Jauréguiberry,

> In just a few years, and with no one paying attention, to not immediately answer one's mobile phone must now be justified. One must explain, get off the hook, even apologize for one's lack of reactivity ... The norm is now to answer one's phone immediately, especially if it's a mobile one. As for e-mails, the norm is now to respond within half a day, or even the hour.[22]

In fact, answering e-mails has become such a burden that, in France, its use for work-related purposes outside of working hours is now mercifully prohibited.

On one average working day of the Spring 2016 semester, I calculated receiving 70 e-mails in a period of 24 hours. Of course, not all were work-related; some were redundant and many were junk mail.[23] Still, e-mail *is* work; it represents an expenditure of time and energy. Every e-mail that lands in my mailbox requires that I spend time on it and make a series of decisions. Is it junk or does it require further attention? If the latter, is it negligible or important? If the latter, can it wait or is it urgent? If it is both important and urgent, what is it? Having reached this classification, I now study the e-mail message for content more closely as I ponder whether, how, from where, when, and to whom I should respond. And, in some cases, even if I decide *not* to respond, I also need to prepare a justification, should I have to provide one. Escaping off the grid for even a short while proves to be a Pyrrhic victory, as the number of e-mails that will accumulate during my absence will require—upon my return—an even more extensive investment of time and energy.

Considering that our personal and professional e-mails are rife with risks of misinterpretation and that they can be stored, retrieved, analyzed, replicated, distributed, and potentially used against us, one can easily appreciate the type of cognitive and emotional labor we must perform in order to respond to all those e-mails that continuously pour in our inboxes and fill them up. Perhaps unsurprisingly, when we receive a text message, "our heart rate increases, blood flow to our skin increases, and 83 percent of us, according to one study, even hold our breath," reports Harris.[24] Rheingold also finds that our breathing patterns change by just opening our e-mail in-box.[25]

And beyond the immediate physiological and neural reactions noted above, this forced labor also prompts a variety of unpleasant social and psychological ones as well. As Joseph Weizenbaum, the creator of the language-processing program ELIZA was dismayed to find, "extremely short exposures to a relatively simple computer program could induce powerful delusional thinking in quite normal adults."[26] As Turkle also notes:

> We come to experience the column of unopened messages in our inboxes as a burden. Then, we project our feelings and worry that our messages are a burden to others … An e-mail or text seems to have been always on its way to the trash … The connected life encourages us to treat those we meet online in something of the same way we treat objects—with dispatch … The self that treats a person as a thing is vulnerable to seeing itself as one.[27]

In order to manage our e-mail messages efficiently and quickly, we must repeatedly establish the sender's identity. How we categorize that identity will then inform our decisions about how to respond. As I discuss below, there is some danger that this sifting-and-dispatching approach to messages will easily replicate in the treatment of the messengers.

Enter_alt_space

Face-work requires *mutual perceptiveness*—my awareness of how you interpret my acts, and how I should interpret yours. However, this aptitude becomes significantly compromised when we interact at the terminal. As e-mail enables a many-to-many communication, the number of messages that circulate necessarily increases, and so do the risks of miscommunication[28] and hence, of face-threatening incidents that disrupt the expressive order. And as those risks increase, we are concurrently less likely to recognize the need to perform face-work than in face-to-face interaction, less motivated and skilled to do so, and less likely to succeed when we do.

Thus, research on cyber-bullying, cyber-incivility, and cyber-ostracism[29] in the workplace find that while terminals have revolutionized our modes of interaction, our need to maintain face has not disappeared, and that our reactions to face-threatening incidents are neither less intense nor less distressing when they occur at the terminal than in face-to-face interaction.[30] It seems that regardless of the setting where we interact, and regardless of whom we are interacting with[31] we typically bring to encounters certain expectations about the reciprocal obligations of face-work, and about our shared responsibility for maintaining the expressive order.[32]

However, when we interact on e-mail, we must adjust to four unfamiliar features of terminal connectivity: *reduced cues, polychronicity, reach,* and *decontextualization/alterability.*[33] Attempting to adjust to these conditions, it is easy to lose one's poise, bearings, balance, or head, and to engage in face-threatening behaviors against self and others. And since we are less likely to perform the routine restorative gestures that repair those unfortunate incidents, the expressive order at the terminal is notoriously volatile and, to quote Rushkoff, not very enjoyable.[34] Below, I review those four features of e-mail connectivity.

Reduced cues

When we interact on e-mail, we can neither communicate nor perceive the kind of information we typically rely on when we interact face-to-face. Here, we are mute, invisible, and literally out of touch. And although we may know—offline—the person with whom we are interacting, we are blind to her proxemics, kinesics, and facial gestures, deaf to her paralanguage and unaware of the contexts from which she communicates. At the terminal, notes Rushkoff, "our experience ... is that of the autistic living with Asperger's syndrome ... a dependence on the verbal over the visual, low pickup on social cues and facial expressions, apparent lack of empathy, and the inability to make eye-contact."[35]

Unsurprisingly, this reduction in information significantly compromises the performance of face-work. For example, Wallace notes that at the terminal "we appear to be less inclined to perform those little civilities common to social interactions"[36] and Turkle suggests that "detaching words from the person uttering them can encourage a certain coarsening."[37] In her research with youth, she also finds that "online communication also offers an opportunity to ignore other people's feelings. You can avoid eye contact. You can elect not to hear how hurt or angry they sound in their voice."[38] Additionally, we often find it difficult to decide whether a message is neutral or sarcastic.[39] We are more likely to misinterpret an ambiguous message as the latter because when we interact on e-mail, we often perceive others (and are perceived) as more hostile and aggressive than in face-to-face encounters.[40] For example, university students interpret what constitutes a too-informal e-mail quite differently than instructors, and the latter react to students' informal tone by liking them less, by evaluating their cognitive aptitudes more negatively, and by being less willing to grant those students even simple requests.[41] Curiously, we also tend to overestimate our ability to both communicate clearly on e-mail and to correctly interpret others' e-mail messages.[42]

When we interpret an e-mail message as face-threatening—as attacking our self-esteem—we often respond in kind[43] thereby triggering rapidly escalating hostile chain reactions.[44] Hence, while e-mail is not necessarily the source of conflicts, it "becomes a much more dangerous tool once conflict has been created."[45] In addition, on e-mail, we are not only more likely to see slights where none were intended, but we are also more prone to "act in uncharacteristic ways ... due to the phenomenon called disinhibition."[46]

Here, we are likely to show "a reduction in concern for self-presentation and the judgment of others,"[47] and "a reduced accountability."[48] As Naquin et al. find, individuals are more likely to lie on e-mail than in face-to-face encounters and to feel that lying is justified.[49] As Aboujaoude also notes,

> Less inhibitions in the virtual world mean that the threshold to act on violent impulses is lower, but so is the threshold to forgive ourselves or other such actions. Desensitizing ourselves to aggression, turning it into entertainment, into something thrilling or even "hot"—these serve to make amoral or violent online manifestations less real than they ought to be. So, besides increasing someone's access to victims, online venues may also provide the person with a psychological out, convincing him that the extreme act will find an understanding audience online, one willing to absolve the perpetrator and pardon the offense.[50]

Moreover, the natural disinclination to witness the shaming of others that Goffman took for granted in face-to-face encounters significantly weakens when individuals interact on e-mail. Thus, Turnage finds that e-mail group members feel less obligated to resolve differences and ease frictions[51] and Wallace finds that they make "fewer remarks that might relieve a tense situation."[52] Invisible, scattered, and benefitting from "diffusion of responsibility,"[53] e-mail users are less willing to perform the face-work that helps sustain each other's faces, to convey recognition, and to protect the terminal expressive order.

The condition of reduced cues we experience on e-mail and other text-based platforms is consequential for other reasons as well. For philosopher Levinas, interaction is central to individuals' experiences of reality, and the ethical dimension of interaction stems from "the sentiment present in the visual perception of a human face."[54] As he explains, "at the sight of a 'face' ... of another person, we have no choice but to feel obligated to help this person immediately and to assist his or her in coping with existential problems."[55] By replacing the human face with faceless messages, terminal connectivity de-faces interactants, de-humanizes them, and obscures the ethical implications of interpersonal encounters. It is, to quote Turkle, "an assault on empathy."[56]

Polychronicity

Because terminal interaction can be *both* synchronous *and* asynchronous, I use the term *polychronous*. While admittedly clunky, it evokes this dual quality. In contrast to face-to-face encounters or phone communication, terminal connectivity enables us to communicate in multiple temporal modes, and this newly gained capability can be quite disorienting to our experience of space and time. For example, I can as easily send the same e-mail to six dispersed people simultaneously, as I can send it in much more elaborate ways: I can send the e-mail to two recipients right now, to two others tomorrow morning, and to two others next week. As another example, three days from now, I will attend to an 'urgent' e-mail you sent me two days ago. Pushing temporal boundaries even further, I can effortlessly combine an e-mail message you sent me four years ago with an e-mail message you sent me today, insert both in an e-mail message I will send you today, and to other people next week. Similarly, of six recipients who receive my e-mail at roughly the same time, some will answer in one minute, some in two days, some in three weeks, and some never will.

The polychronicity of e-mail and other such platforms also fosters the experience of omnipresence—the extraordinary ability to transmit any passing thought, emotion, or desire whenever, from wherever, and to whomever. While this affordance has now become taken-for-granted, it is unique in human history and psychology, to say nothing of politics. It is radically re-coding the rules of interaction, both at the terminal and away from it, and with frequent negative outcomes. For example, e-mail enables us to com-municate on impulse and, typically, with an implied expectation of immediate reply.[57] But when or whether the other will respond is unpredictable. Thus, not only are we more likely to misinterpret an ambiguous message as face-threatening, we are also likely to misinterpret a silence in similar ways.[58] After all, in face-to-face encounters, we expect that *when* we communicate to another, this other at the very least acknowledges *that* we have communic-ated and have been heard. As Goffman puts it,

> By saying something, the speaker opens himself up to the possibility that the intended recipients will affront him by not listening … And should he meet with such a reception, he will find himself committed to the necessity of taking face-saving action against them.[59]

However, while in face-to-face encounters, we would likely interpret the other's failure to acknowledge our communicative act as an overt and calcu-lated affront, such potentially face-threatening incidents are frequent in ter-minal interactions, and their causes can be merely technical.

This silence is important. Wesselmann and Williams report that the experience of ostracism thwarts the four fundamental needs of belonging, self-esteem, control, and meaningful existence. As a denial of social recog-nition, the physical effects of ostracism include increase in blood pressure and the activation of "the part of the brain involved in experiencing physical pain."[60] As researchers also find, the noxious effects of ostracism in the workplace are worse than those resulting from harassment.[61] These effects do not disappear at the terminal. For example, respondents in a research conducted by Privitera and her team report that such terminal silences are a major form of cyber-incivility.[62] Roberts et al. find that indi-viduals report discomfort and anxiety when they do not receive instant feedback in their terminal interactions,[63] and Williams et al. find that the effects of (even mis-perceived) cyber-ostracism can be psychologically quite unsettling—even when the perpetrator is but a computer program.[64] More troublesome, those emotions then shape the ostracized person's offline behaviors, often in undesirable ways. Hence, the perplexing power of omnipresence must uneasily coexist with unpredictable and unexplainable silences, which we often misinterpret as indicating lack of recognition, dismissal, ostracism, ex-*communication*.

Reach

In contrast to face-to-face encounters that are typically fleeting, contained to the time and place of their occurrence, and oriented to a small number of physically co-present others, at the terminal our transmissions acquire a reach that is both unfathomable and beyond our control. As Baym and boyd note,[65] this reach is spatial and temporal. Spatial, because I can communicate instantly with a large number of scattered individuals, regardless of our respective physical location. Temporal, because what I spontaneously communicate right now in this type of connectivity is stored, is retrievable, and is therefore permanent.[66]

This new experience of inconceivable reach requires that we continuously resolve a number of disconnects. The first one pertains to the fleeting and spontaneous words we are prompted to communicate at the terminal and the permanent traces those leave behind. This is especially the case when we communicate with each other at the terminal in a near-synchronous rhythm. In those instances when the rhythm simulates a spontaneous and 'live' conversation, we experience the words we write as fleeting, emergent, and existing only in the moment of their creation and transmission. In terminal connectivity, however, those words take on a permanence—a materiality— that we never intended. As Rushkoff puts it,

> It's not just the line between public and private activity that has vanished, but the distance between now and then. The past is wound up into the present and no longer at an appropriate or even predictable scale ... Nothing, no matter how temporally remote is off-limits. A forgotten incident can resurface into the present like an explosion, threatening one's reputation, job, or marriage.[67]

And while we typically expect the spontaneous faux-pas we commit in live conversations to be overlooked, kept private, forgiven, and forgotten, 'the net never forgets.'

The terminal form of connectivity forces us to also resolve a second disconnect between the relative privacy, invisibility, and anonymity of our activities and their publicness, visibility, and traceability. Thus, while we might access the terminal from the privacy of our house, every word we communicate there can become quickly public and visible. This disconnect is also quite unique in human psychology, and as the nightly news cease-lessly remind us, those who are a bit too careless in managing this dis-connect can suffer punishments that seem sometimes disproportionately swift and severe.

Decontextualization/alterability

The terminal type of connectivity also requires us to resolve the disconnect between *situatedness* and *decontextualization*. Thus, although we typically experience many terminal interactions as unique, situation-specific, and invit-ing a context-appropriate response, we must constantly mind the risk that our responses can be extracted from their contexts, re-contextualized, and even altered. And if the very extraction of a communicative act from its context already distorts its meaning, its 'viral' dissemination across contexts amplifies this distortion in nano-seconds. As the current investigation about the role of 'fake news' on social media in the recent election attests, this feature of e-mail interaction is not only detrimental to interpersonal relations, but to inter-national ones as well.

Whenever we interact with others on e-mail, the fleeting words we impulsively express leave permanent records in countless digital memories. The private words we intend to convey to a few chosen others can become embarrassingly public. The context-specific words we compose can be decontextualized, reproduced, and altered. These disconnects are especially significant when what we write reveals information that we carefully monitor in face-to-face encounters. We monitor it precisely because we anticipate the face-threatening consequences for failing to do so, and because a face-to-face encounter is a mutually attuning dance where participants coordinate the appropriate level, context, audience, and timing of self-disclosure.[68] This is what face-work partly entails. Terminal users may certainly try to coordinate this dance, but they must do so by relying on a mode of interaction that is unfamiliar, destabilizing, and disorienting. Here, anything we express takes on face-threatening dynamics that immediately escape our understanding and control.

No longer restricted by the spatial, temporal, and physical parameters that have traditionally limited our impulse to communicate, we can both manifest ourselves spontaneously and simultaneously to large numbers of scattered individuals, but under conditions of 'collapsed context' where "it is particu-larly challenging to understand 'who is out there and when' and raises the potential for greater misalignment between imagined and actual audiences."[69] In such conditions, the terminal is also a social minefield where the constant threat of "mutually assured humiliation is only a few clicks away,"[70] and where "everyone can be turned into an informer."[71] As Aboujaoude also notes, the terminal gives us "new tools to uncover unpleasantness about one another, even as it increases the likelihood of such unpleasantness occurring in the first place."[72]

Restore

Face-to-face encounters always present the risk of face-threatening incidents that may damage self-esteem. When those occur, we routinely perform restorative gestures that reinstate participants' faces and sustain the expressive order. These gestures are especially important when threats to face are made publicly. If we typically find it unpleasant to lose face in front of just one person, this reaction is considerably intensified when we lose face in front of many. Since we often send e-mails simultaneously to many scattered individuals and since addressees are more likely to misinterpret our transmissions as face-threatening, it does not seem unreasonable to expect that restorative gestures would be especially well-honed in e-mail interactions. However, the exact opposite obtains. Here, we are less likely to recognize those instances when restorative gestures are warranted, less motivated and skilled to perform them, and less successful when we try. There are several reasons explaining this deterioration.

First, Goffman implied that restorative gestures took place *live, in situ,* and through the coordinated efforts of mutually aware and physically co-present participants—a victim, an offender, and an audience. As Cupach and Metts, for example, document, restorative gestures are more effective when they are immediate and visible:

> The nonverbal display of anxiety or discomfort can function much like an apology insofar as it demonstrates to others that the offending person acknowledges the impropriety of his or her behavior. Merely appearing to be chagrined (by blushing or grimacing) can show one's self-effacement and thereby mitigate negative attributions that might be ascribed by observers.[73]

However, because it is rather difficult to convey and perceive such non-verbal gestures at the terminal, it becomes near-impossible to sense whether restorative gestures are warranted, performed, and if so, whether they are successful.

Second, restorative gestures are much more difficult to perform at the terminal because connectivity there is often polychromous and can be both private and public. In such conditions, those who witness a face-threatening incident might not be those who observe restorative gestures and vice-versa. For example, members of a team might simultaneously witness—at their individual terminals—the purposeful degradation of a colleague, but the perpetrator performs restorative gestures much later, over multiple messages that s/he shares with only a few recipients. In such conditions, team members who witnessed the face-threatening incident might no longer remember (or care about) it when the offender performs said restorative gestures. Conversely, team members who might not have directly witnessed the face-threatening incident might be puzzled (or irritated) when they become the captive audience of those restorative gestures that the perpetrator performs at the terminal. For example, Hastings' research finds that office employees were embarrassed:

> when another employee was "publicly" criticized through e-mail. In those cases, feelings of being drawn into a conflict where they did not belong were described, and they felt embarrassed for the person confronted as well as embarrassed for the person sending the confrontational e-mail ...[74]

Worse yet, Turkle remarks that the very attempt to perform restorative gestures at the terminal might be counterproductive: "E-mail tends to go back and forth without resolution. Misunderstandings are frequent. Feelings get hurt. And the greater the misunderstanding, the greater the number of e-mails, far more than necessary."[75] As face-threatening incidents proliferate and remain unresolved, connectivity is punctuated by bruised feelings, angry outbursts, and punishing silences.[76]

Inter-face-work

Elsewhere, I have developed the concept of *inter-face-work* to refer to a mode of attention that should facilitate our interactions with others at the terminal.[77] More than just applying 'netiquette' rules, this mode of attention helps us intuitively compensate for the distinctive limitations imposed by e-mail interaction, intelligently regulate the new powers it bestows, and successfully avoid the new categories of risks it presents us. Overall, most of these limitations, powers, and risks pertain to interactants' faces—the need for social recognition. At first glance, it might seem that the wounds to self-esteem inflicted by verbal assaults in terminal confrontations are less painful than the bruises to the body inflicted by physical attacks in corporal ones. However, the distinction between those two realms of experience is less clear than once believed. As Honneth emphasizes, "the experience of social degradation and humiliation jeopardizes the identity of human beings to the same degrees as the suffering of illness jeopardizes their physical well-being."[78]

Browse and shuffle, drag and drop, trash and block. As complex as it is to satisfy the need for recognition when we interact face-to-face, the rules that encode e-mail interaction seem designed to thwart this essential need and to impair the process whereby users can gratify it. While conveying recognition and esteem requires focused attention, the terminal's "new dominant attention paradigm of always on, anywhere, anytime, any place consists of split-screen, continual partial attention."[79] While conveying esteem entails timely responsiveness, terminal connectivity prompts "a 'semi-sync' communication where everybody is 'pausable' and can be delayed."[80] Interacting in this way, the terminal self is both more likely to passively deny esteem to others, but also to vociferously declare them as unworthy of it. As the rising number of hateful websites, trolls, tweets, and

Facebook posts attests, terminal connectivity seems to encourage what Aboujaoude calls an 'everyday viciousness.'[81] As he notes,

> if logging on begins as an attempt to fulfill our human need for self-expression and connectedness, it often gives voice to some less mature and antisocial impulses, aspects of ourselves that have historically been kept in check by culture, expectation, religion, and what one might call the social contract.[82]

Aboujaoude's clinical impressions are supported by a recent Pew research that finds "73% of adult internet users have seen someone be harassed in some way online, 60% said they had witnessed someone being called offensive names, 53% had seen efforts to purposefully embarrass someone, 25% had seen someone being physically threatened, 24% witnessed someone being harassed for a sustained period of time," and 40 percent have personally experienced online harassment.[83] And while frequent face-threatening incidents might seem ephemeral and limited to their terminal manifestations, turning off our devices does not magically erase their effects. On the contrary, Waldvogel points out that how members of an organization interact at the terminal is shaped by, and will shape that organization's culture.[84]

For Goffman, face-work was the very *condition* of interaction and the basic mechanism protecting the expressive order. Because face-threatening incidents can destabilize that order and paralyze interaction, all participants in an encounter are expected to play their parts by performing avoidance and restorative gestures. Accordingly, *inter-face-work* is as important to terminal interaction as face-work is to face-to-face. But because our inter-face-work skills are typically so poorly developed, terminal encounters can easily derail in face-threatening incidents. Mistaking social recognition for positively rewarded visibility, the terminal self must find the repeated experience of public shaming combined with punishing silence particularly upsetting.

How users interact at the terminal also disrupts the expressive order because they must now spend an inordinate amount of time and energy trying to repair at the terminal, face-to-face, and sometimes both—those multiplying incidents. And even when unfortunate incidents have been resolved for all practical purposes—an unlikely event—there will remain a negative emotional "surplus-value," a sort of *rancoeur*. These negative emotions can easily set the tone for subsequent terminal encounters and will contaminate face-to-face ones as well. For Paul Virilio, the present condition of connectivity is a form of 'radioactivity.'[85] As Williams also remarks, our society is increasingly populated by angry individuals

> who feel they have the right, the authority and the need not only to comment on everything, but to make sure their voice is heard above the rest, and to drag down any opposing views through personal attacks, loud repetition and confrontation.[86]

By corrupting the satisfaction of the need for social recognition, terminal connectivity can easily destabilize users' relations with others, fail to mobilize their commitment to the expressive order, and weaken the networks that— they are often promised—replace a nostalgic 'community.' While the frequent experience of non-recognition at the terminal might seem a benign and ephemeral micro-phenomenon, Honneth suggests that class conflicts can also be understood as struggles for social recognition—struggles that take on different forms in different historical periods and social groups.[87] And while terminal connectivity cannot be blamed for the emergence of entropic social or political trends, it still contributes to them. By multiplying the risks of face-threatening incidents and by inhibiting the opportunities to resolve them, it frustrates the need for social recognition and degrades users' ability to develop and practice those skills such as mutual perceptiveness, negotiation, and conflict-resolution. Impaired in such ways, the terminal self becomes less skilled in resisting and more vulnerable to domination, the topic of next chapter.

Notes

1 This chapter both adapts and develops ideas presented in a book I published in Italian (see Gottschalk 2015).
2 Shipley and Schwalbe (2008), 249.
3 Pariser (2011), 11.
4 Goffman (1955), 215.
5 Bauman (2005), 21.
6 Goffman (1955), 216.
7 Goffman (1955), 215. As many historical examples amply demonstrate, entire categories of individuals can find their faces suddenly and violently withdrawn, not because of behaviors that prove them unworthy, but because of changing social norms.
8 Goffman (1955), 219.
9 Ibid.
10 Gardner (2006), 29.
11 As the scholars associated with the Palo Alto School have convincingly suggested, negative communicative acts can have devastating effects in a person's mind, in small groups, in institutions, and in international relations (see especially Winkin (1981); Wittezele and Garcia (1992)).
12 Blanchard (2004).
13 Suler; quoted in Riva and Galimberti (2001), 105.
14 Ling (2010); see also Turkle (2011).
15 See especially Baruch (2005); Lim and Thompson (2009).
16 Purcell (2011).
17 Purcell and Rainie (2014), 2.
18 Rainie and Wellman (2012), 65.
19 Gitlin (2011), 211.
20 Carr (2011).
21 Czerwinski, Horvitz, and Wilhite (2004).
22 Jauréguiberry (2014), 30.
23 On the other hand, this number does not include the pop-up messages that appear on the terminal when I browse websites, read the news, and other sudden messages that often ask me to react in some form.

24 Harris (2014), 169.
25 Rheingold (2012).
26 Carr (2011), 205. This quote refers to the pioneering ELIZA computer program that mimicked simplistic conversations with users.
27 Turkle (2011), 268.
28 See especially Hastings (2009); Kanungo and Jain (2008); Shipley and Schwalbe (2008); Turnage (2008).
29 Those terms are often used interchangeably to refer to face-threatening incidents that happen online.
30 Wesselmann and Williams (2011), 128–129.
31 By "whomever" I am referring to those cases where we assume that the person with whom we are interacting is a rational and sane human being who shares key cultural norms and values of interaction.
32 See especially Baruch (2005); Lim and Thompson (2009); Friedman and Currall (2003); Priviteria and Campbell (2009).
33 Some of those concepts have been suggested by Baym and boyd (2012). Baym also discusses qualities such as mobility, permanence, interactivity, and storage. I have adapted or extended the other terms I use to discuss the unique features of terminal connectivity.
34 Rushkoff (2011), 35–36.
35 Rushkoff (2011), 92.
36 Wallace (1999), 17.
37 Turkle (2011), 236.
38 Turkle (2011), 184.
39 O'Sullivan and Flannagin (2003).
40 See especially Giumetti et al. (2012); Kurtzberg, Naquin, and Belkin (2005); Naquin, Kurtzberg, and Belkin (2008 and 2010).
41 Stephens, Houser, and Cowan (2009).
42 Kruger et al. (2005).
43 King and Moreggi (2007).
44 Friedman and Currall (2003).
45 Turnage (2008).
46 Suler, quoted in Riva and Galimberti (2001).
47 Joinson (2007).
48 Wallace (1999); see also Aboujaoude (2011).
49 Naquin, Kurtzberg, and Belkin (2008).
50 Aboujaoude (2011), 111.
51 Ibid.
52 Wallace (1999), 17.
53 Darley and Latané (1968).
54 Honneth (2007), 119.
55 Ibid.
56 Turkle (2015).
57 Derks and Bakker (2010).
58 Kalman and Rafaeli (2011).
59 Goffman (1955), 227.
60 Wesselmann and Williams (2011), 128–129.
61 O'Reilly et al. (2015).
62 Privitera and Campbell (2009).
63 Roberts (2014), 133.
64 Williams, Cheung, and Choi (2000); see also Giumetti et al. (2012).
65 Those concepts have been adapted from those suggested by Baym and boyd (2012). Baym also discusses qualities such as mobility, permanence, interactivity, and storage.

66 Mayer-Schonberger (2011).
67 Rushkoff (2013), 157.
68 Domenici and Littlejohn (2006).
69 Baym and boyd (2012), 323; see also Marwick and boyd (2010).
70 Rainie and Wellman (2012), 301.
71 Turkle (2011), 261.
72 Aboujaoude (2011), 90.
73 Cupach and Metts (1994), 10.
74 Hastings (2009), 41.
75 Turkle (2011), 167.
76 As Lim and Thompson (2009) report, men and women use different face-threatening
    strategies on e-mail.
77 Gottschalk (2015).
78 Honneth (1992), 192.
79 Rheingold (2012), 56.
80 Turkle (2011), 161.
81 Aboujaoude (2011).
82 Aboujaoude (2011), 21.
83 Duggan (2014).
84 Waldvogel (2007).
85 Virilio, Kittler, and Armitage (1999), 83.
86 Williams (2014).
87 See especially Scheff (2000) and Hochschild (2016).

References

Aboujaoude, Elias. 2011. *Virtually You: The Dangerous Powers of the E-Personality*. New
    York: W. W. Norton & Co.
Baruch, Yehuda. 2005. "Bullying on the Net: Adverse Behavior on E-mail and its
    Impact." *Information and Management* 42: 361–371.
Bauman, Zygmunt. 2005. *Liquid Life*. Cambridge, UK: Polity.
Baym, Nancy K. and danah boyd. 2012. "Socially Mediated Publicness: An Intro-
    duction." *Journal of Broadcasting & Electronic Media* 56(3): 320–329.
Blanchard, Anita. 2004. "Virtual Behavior Settings: An Application of Behavior
    Setting Theories to Virtual Communities." *Journal of Computer-Mediated Communi-
    cation* 9(2).
Carr, Nicholas. 2011. *The Shallows: What the Internet is Doing to Our Brains*. New
    York: W. W. Norton & Co.
Cupach, William R. and Sandra Metts. 1994. *Face-work*. Thousand Oaks, CA: Sage.
Czerwinski, Mary, Eric Horvitz, and Susan Wilhite. 2004. "A Diary Study of Task
    Switching and Interruptions." Proceedings of the SIGCHI Conference on Human
    Factors in Computing Systems. New York: ACM.
Darley, John. M. and Bibb Latané. 1968. "Bystander Intervention in Emergencies:
    Diffusion of Responsibility." *Journal of Personality and Social Psychology* 8: 377–383.
Derks, Daantje and Arnold B. Bakker. 2010. "The Impact of E-Mail Communication
    on Organizational Life." *Cyberpsychology: Journal of Psychosocial Research on Cyberspace*
    4(1). Retrieved December 12, 2013. file://localhost/(http://cyberpsychology.
    eu:view.php%3Fcisloclanku=2010052401&article=1).
Domenici, Kathy and Stephen W. Littlejohn. 2006. *Face-work: Bridging Theory and
    Practice*. Thousand Oaks, CA: Sage.

Friedman, Raymond and Steven C. Currall. 2003. "Conflict Escalation: Dispute Exacerbating Elements of E-mail Communication." *Human Relations* 56(11): 1325–1347.

Gardner, Howard. 2006. *Changing Minds*. Boston: Harvard Business School Press.

Gitlin, Todd. 2011. "Nomadicity." pp. 207–214, in *The Digital Divide: Arguments for and Against Facebook, Google, Texting, and the Age of Social Networking*, Mark Bauerlein (ed.). New York: Jeremy P. Tarcher.

Giumetti, Gary W., Eric S. McKibben, Andrea L Hatfield, Amber N. Schroeder, and Robin M. Kowalski. 2012. "Cyberincivility @ Work: The New Age of Interpersonal Deviance." *Cyberpsychology, Behavior and Social Networking* 15(3): 148–154.

Goffman, Erving. 1955. "On Face-Work: An Analysis of Ritual Elements in Social Interaction." *Psychiatry* 18(3): 213–231.

Gottschalk. Simon. 2015. *Interfacework: l'interazione simbolica nell'epoca digitale* [Inter-Face-Work: Symbolic Interaction in the Digital Age]. Introduction by Giuseppina Cerosimo. Calimera, Italy: Edizioni Kurumuny.

Harris, Michael. 2014. *The End of Absence: Reclaiming What We've Lost in a World of Constant Connection*. NY: Current.

Hastings, Sally O. 2009. "Embarrassing E-mails in Organizations: Exploring Online Embarrassment and Identity Management." *Journal of Creative Communications* 4(1): 33–43.

Hochschild, Arlie R. 2016. *Strangers in Their Own Land: Anger and Mourning on the American Right*. New York: New Press.

Honneth, Axel. 1992. "Integrity and Disrespect: Principles of a Conception of Morality Based on the Theory of Recognition." *Political Theory* 29(2): 187–201.

Honneth, Axel. 2007. *Disrespect: The Normative Foundations of Critical Theory*. Cambridge, UK: Polity.

Jauréguiberry, Francis. 2014. "La Déconnection aux Technologies de Communication." *La Découverte-Réseaux* 186(4): 15–49.

Joinson, Adam, N. 2007. "Disinhibition and the Internet." pp. 43–60 in *Psychology and the Internet: Intrapersonal, Interpersonal, and Transpersonal Implications*, J. Gayckenback (ed.). Burlington, MA: Elsevier.

Kalman, Yoram and Sheizaf Rafaeli. 2011. "Online Pauses and Silence: Chronemic Expectancy Violations in Written Computer-Mediated Communication." *Communication Research* 38(1): 54–69.

Kanungo, Shiraj and Vikas Jain. 2008. "Modeling Email Use: A Case of Email System Transition." *Systems Dynamics Review* 24(3): 299–319.

King, Storm A. and Danielle Moreggi. 2007. "Internet Self-Help and Support Groups: The Pros and Cons of Text-Based Mutual Aid." pp. 221–244 in *Psychology and the Internet: Intrapersonal, Interpersonal, and Transpersonal Implications*, J. Gayckenback (ed.). Burlington, MA: Elsevier.

Kruger, Justin, Nicholas Epley, Jason Parker, and Zhi-Wen Ng. 2005. "Egocentrism over E-mail: Can we Communicate as well as we Think?" *Journal of Personality and Social Psychology* 89(6): 925–936.

Kurtzberg, Terri R., Charles E. Naquin, and Liuba Y. Belkin. 2005. "Electronic Performance Appraisals: The Effects of E-mail Communication on Peer Ratings in Actual and Simulated Environments." *Organizational Behavior and Human Decision Processes* 98(2): 216–226.

Lim, Vivien K. G. and Teo Thompson. 2009. "Mind Your E-Manners: Impact of Cyber- Incivility on Employees' Work Attitudes and Behaviors." *Information and Management* 46: 419–425.

Ling, Rich. 2010. "Texting as a Life Phase Medium." *Journal of Computer-Mediated Communication* 15: 277–292.

Marwick, Alice and danah boyd. 2010. "I Tweet Honestly, I Tweet Passionately: Twitter Users, Context Collapse, and the Imagined Audience." *New Media & Society* 13(1): 114–133.

Mayer-Schonberger, Viktor. 2011. *Delete: The Virtue of Forgetting in the Digital Age.* Princeton, NJ: Princeton University Press.

Naquin, Charles E., Terri R. Kurtzberg, and Liuba Y. Belkin. 2008. "E-mail Communication and Group Cooperation in Mixed Motive Contexts." *Social Justice Research* 21(4): 470–489.

Naquin, Charles E., Terri R. Kurtzberg, and Liuba Y. Belkin. 2010. "The Finer Points of Lying Online: E-mail versus Pen and Paper." *Journal of Applied Psychology* 95(2): 387–394.

O'Reilly, Jane, Sandra L. Robinson, Jennifer L. Berdahl, and Sara Banki. 2015. "Is Negative Attention Better Than No Attention? The Comparative Effects of Ostracism and Harassment at Work." *Organization Science* 26(3): 774–793.

O'Sullivan, Patrick B. and Andrew J. Flannagin. 2003. "Reconceptualizing 'Flaming' and Other Problematic Messages." *New Media and Society* 5: 69–94.

Pariser, Eli. 2012. *The Filter Bubble: How the New Personalized Web Is Changing What We Read and How We Think.* New York: Penguin.

Privitera, Carmel and Mary Ann Campbell. 2009. "Cyberbullying: The New Face of Workplace Bullying." *CyberPsychology & Behavior* 12(4): 395–400.

Purcell, Kristen and Lee Rainie. 2014. "Technology's Impact on Workers." Pew Research Center. 2014. Retrieved on February 20, 2017. www.pewinternet. org/2014/12/30/technologys-impact-on-workers/.

Purcell, Kristen. 2011. "Search and E-mail Still Top the List of Most Popular Online Activities." Pew Research Center. 2011. Retrieved December 23, 2013. www. pewinternet.org/Reports/2011/Search-and-e-mail.aspx.

Rainie, Lee and Barry Wellman. 2012. *Networked: The New Social Operating System.* Cambridge, MA: MIT Press.

Rheingold, Howard. 2012. *NetSmart: How To Thrive Online.* Cambridge, MA: MIT Press.

Riva, Giuseppe and Carlo Galimberti (eds.). 2001. *Towards CyberPsychology: Mind, Cognition and Society in the Internet Age.* Amsterdam: IOS.

Roberts, Paul. 2014. *The Impulse Society: America in the Age of Instant Gratification.* New York: Bloomsberry.

Rushkoff, Douglas. 2013. *Present Shock: When Everything Happens Now.* New York: Penguin.

Scheff, Thomas J. 2000. *Emotions, Nationalism, and War.* Lincoln, NE: iUniverse.

Shipley, David and Will Schwalbe. 2008. *Send: Why People E-mail So Badly and How To Do It Better.* New York: Vantage.

Stephens, Keri K., Marian L. Houser, and Renee L. Cowan. 2009. "R U Able to MeatMe?: The Impact of Students' Overly Casual E-mail Messages to Instructors." *Communication Education* 58(3): 303–326.

Turkle, Sherry. 2011. *Alone Together: Why We Demand More of Technology and Less of Each Other.* New York: Basic Books.

Turkle, Sherry. 2015. *Reclaiming Conversation: The Power of Talk in the Digital Age.* New York: Penguin.

Turnage, Anna K. 2008. "Email Flaming Behavior and Organizational Conflict." *Journal of Computer Mediated Communication* 13: 43–59.

Virilio, Paul, Friedrich Kittler, and John Armitage. 1999. "The Information Bomb: A Conversation." *Angelaki: Journal of the Theoretical Humanities*, 4(2): 81–90. http://dx.doi.org/10.1080/09697259908572036.

Waldvogel, Joan. 2007. "Greetings and Closings in Workplace E-mail." *Journal of Computer-Mediated Communication* 12: 456–477.

Wallace, Patricia. 1999. *The Psychology of the Internet.* Cambridge University Press.

Wesselmann, Eric D. and Kipling D. Williams. 2011. "Being Ignored and Excluded in Electronic-Based Interactions." pp. 127–144 in *Strategic Uses of Social Technology: An Interactive Perspective of Social Psychology*, Zachary Birchmeier, Beth Dietz-Uhler, and Garold Stasser (eds.). Cambridge University Press.

Williams, Kipling D., Christopher K. T. Cheung, and Wilma Choi. 2000. "Cyberostracism: Effects of Being Ignored over the Internet." *Journal of Personality and Social Psychology* 79(5): 748–762.

Williams, Ray. 2014. "The Cult of Ignorance in the United States: Anti-Intellectualism and the 'Dumbing Down' of America." psychologytoday.com. Retrieved June 7, 2014.

Winkin, Yves. 1981. *La Nouvelle Communication.* Paris: éditions du Seuil.

Wittezele, Jean-Jacques and Teresa Garcia. 1992. *A La Recherche de L'école de Palo Alto.* Paris: éditions du Seuil.

7   Submit

"We know where you are. We know where you have been. We can more or less know what you're thinking about."[1] A fifth terminal default setting is its multiplying capacities for surveillance—the collection, storage, retrieval, distribution, manipulation, and use of private information. Completely obliterating our fundamental right to privacy and transforming how we understand and experience it, the new terminal capacities for surveillance require our attention because they transfer an enormous amount of power to (not always benevolent) organizations such as state agencies (foreign or domestic), commercial enterprises, the workplace, health-providing institutions, etc. Shoshana Zuboff calls this new form of power in surveillance capitalism the 'Big Other,' As she explains:

> It is constituted by unexpected and often illegible mechanisms of extraction, commodification, and control that effectively exile persons from their own behavior while producing new markets of behavioral prediction and modification. Surveillance capitalism challenges democratic norms and departs in key ways from the centuries long evolution of market capitalism.[2]

"Google knows more about us than we can remember ourselves," writes Viktor Mayer-Schönberger.[3] "It knows us so well that it finishes our sentences," remarks Lynch.[4] In contrast to our handling of pre-terminal technologies, our activities at the terminal are constantly recorded. As an example, up until quite recently, activities such as buying anything, reading a newspaper, listening to music, looking at pictures, watching a movie, consulting a website, locating an address on a map, or playing a video-game, were dispersed, anonymous, private, and unrecorded. Today, all those activities occur on the same terminals, can be precisely located, timed, attributed to a specific individual, stored, made public, and shared. More worrisome, it has now become cliché to remark that even when our terminal is turned off, it is constantly collecting and transmitting information about where we are, where we have been, for how long, etc. The most baffling aspect of this situation is not the terminal's surveillance capacities, as daunting as they are, but that it has become cliché. In other words, we willingly consent to a condition of constant and remote surveillance that—except in spy movies or paranoid delusions—would have been considered preposterous a mere few decades ago. In the hypermodern moment, however, "intense scrutiny—even in unexpected situations—is a realistic possibility" and "transparency is a new requirement."[5] As Van Brakel et al. note,

> It can be argued that we are living in an era of statistical, algorithmic or pre-emptive surveillance whereby the predictive analysis and pattern recognition by intelligent algorithms of big or small unstructured or structured data is leading to whole new sorting mechanisms and actionable profiles, which pose a new plethora of old and new issues.[6]

Sociologist Ragnedda points out that in contemporary society, the two organs of the surveillance apparatus are the state and the corporation. Both collect private information for different reasons and use it differently. The state records and threatens, the corporation observes and seduces. The state relies on the gaze, the corporation relies on language and images. While the state has still a monopoly on the legal use of violence and coercion, it is the private corporation—rather than public institutions—that propagates the norms, values, and principles that define contemporary society. As a result, the distinction between the political and the economic spheres has collapsed: "A good citizen/consumer is, by definition, well integrated into social life, exhibiting predictable behavior that conforms to the general needs of contemporary consumer-oriented social relations … a good consumer is also a good citizen, and vice-versa."[7]

"Personal data is the new oil of the Internet and the new currency of the digital world," suggests Meglena Kuneva, the European Consumer commissioner.[8] Indeed, a variety of commercial and other enterprises are busy analyzing the information we produce about ourselves at the terminal—click after click, aware and unaware, intentionally and not—to seduce us with products, services, or ideas, to channel our desires along certain paths, to activate particular emotions, and to delineate our opportunities. That is, to quote Ragnedda, the *corporate* version of surveillance. Organized according to a different logic, however, this very same information can also be used to intimidate, threaten, manipulate, and coerce us. That is the *strong state* version of surveillance. However, as all the protections of our privacy are being violently shattered, the demographic and biographic information we have been forced to surrender at the terminals of health, employment, educational, financial, and other official institutions (state surveillance) are cross-referenced with the psychometric information we have been seduced to transmit at the fun and personalized terminals of sociability, entertainment, and consumption (corporate surveillance). The first type of information can be used to threaten our physical well-being; the second, to manipulate our psychosocial one. Examining the structure of the 'surveillance-industrial complex,' Fuchs warns that "the world's most powerful state institutions have collaborated with the world's most powerful communications companies to implement totalitarian surveillance systems."[9]

In Italy, Ragnedda finds that students "completely underestimate the danger of privacy violation and the transfer of personal data."[10] In the US, Turkle reports that young people react to this erosion of privacy with despair, hopelessness, anxiety, or plain denial. And even those lucid enough to attempt to appraise the situation head-on have abdicated to the realization that there is simply no alternative.[11] And in contrast to Erikson's famous insight that youth constitutes a sort of moratorium, Turkle remarks that "we see a first generation going through adolescence knowing that their every misstep, all awkward gestures of their youth, are being frozen in a computer's memory."[12]

In France, Acquisiti discovers that when it comes to matter of privacy at the terminal, adult consumers defy traditional psychological models of rational behavior. Calling such models 'unrealistic,' he proposes to replace them by more complex ones that are based on *psychological distortion*. Those, he believes, will hopefully provide a more accurate understanding of consumers' decision-making:

> Even individuals who genuinely want to protect their private lives are unable to do so because of psychological distortions … We have emphasized that these distortions affect naïve individuals as well as more savvy ones. We were surprised to notice that those inconsistencies can occur even when individuals correctly perceive the risks to their private lives.[13]

Perhaps one reason explaining our consent to this outrageous situation is that this constant surveillance does not feel as concrete, constraining, and coercive as Bentham's panopticon and other such conspicuous forms. On the contrary, hypermodern surveillance is "soft,"[14] "remote and silent,"[15] "intrusive and invisible, more invasive but perceived as normal."[16] Comparing a Big Brother type of surveillance to the current one, Levy notes that:

> Facebook—or more precisely the economic social order of which Facebook represents an example and for which Facebook provides a perfect figure—is all light: a mirthful celebration of individuality and expression … Facebook is a bright, facilitating presence, which wins adherents by making its ideological function as subtle as possible.[17]

We also comply because we are seduced by the terminal's personalized promises of instant pleasure, performativity, and power we'll enjoy if we agree to complete transparency. When, as Bauman remarks, "the fear of disclosure has been stifled by the joy of being noticed,"[18] the terminal is an especially effective mechanism of (self-imposed) surveillance and social control. We also consent to constant surveillance because doing so does not seem like that big of a deal and because, we are told, millions of other consumers just like us don't seem to mind and are happy with their decision to 'register' and 'become a member.'

Accept terms

This consent to constant surveillance, however, is a myth. We no longer have a choice; we do not consent but submit. Although we increasingly find our-selves forced to interact with a terminal to access an exponentially growing array of resources, in many cases, we can only do so if we first 'accept' or 'agree' with the terms of incomprehensible contracts, and provide private information to faceless entities. If we agree with the terms, we can proceed and access the desired resources. If we 'decline' we will find our 'access denied.' To make matters worse, the terms of the 'contracts' we are forced to agree to are not only incomprehensible to most users but, as Pariser notes, often also contain the clause that its authors "reserve the right to change the rules of the game at any time," even retroactively.[19] As Fuchs notes, the cor-porate privacy policies and terms of social media use "tend to assure the users that they deal with user data responsibly, but at the same time define and enable consumer privacy violations so that these terms and policies become ideological documents."[20]

Pervasive and non-negotiable, this soft surveillance appears to "gain com-pliance by persuasion, rather than coercion, but still denies the individuals any meaningful choice in the matter."[21] As Lynch put it, by abolishing our right to privacy, by denying us the right to choose, "the terminal has decided for us."[22] In this situation, "windows on the world become windows on the indi-vidual, and the individual is not guaranteed to realize they are on display."[23] At the same time, research suggest that individuals who realize that their privacy has been exposed without their consent experience "emotional, psy-choanalytic and corporeal responses which are sometimes stultifyingly pro-found."[24] And one can safely assume that those intense responses are not confined to their terminal manifestations. Ragnedda also notes that the false sense of choice or agency we experience when we surrender our privacy rights to the terminal easily neutralizes the anxieties that inevitably surface when confronting the complete collapse of the private sphere.

This form of extortion is often dehumanizing and unwarranted. If the coercive extraction of private information was imposed solely in those instances when individuals accessed the terminal to buy something, one could perhaps justify that such imposition is necessary to improve inventory-management and delivery. However, we must also 'agree' to this violation of privacy when we use the terminal to simply interact with others, look up information, locate ourselves on a GPS, and perform other relatively simple and routine activities. And while politicians and journalists are quick to sensationalize dramatic instances of cyber-bullying among teen-agers or cyber-sexcapades among public figures, they remain curiously silent about this constant electronic stalking—this new form of psychological intimidation that targets virtually everyone, including in the privacy of our homes.[25]

Capitulation to permanent surveillance also invites a certain relationship to authority, which sociologist Dubey characterizes as "a blend of culpability, of panic, of a feeling of inferiority, and eventually, of submission."[26] Of course, we can expend the time, resources, and energy necessary to deploy various strategies that will prevent or minimize some of the new risks inherent in living with a complete lack of privacy. After all, even Mark Zuckerberg covers the camera eye of his laptop with a post-it. But this lack is now the new (and paranoid) 'normal.'

Verify your identity

"I just verified your home address on Google, and it matches the information you submitted," announces Theresa, a loan officer at the bank. In contrast to other historical periods, today we must be prepared that—at any moment—the person we are about to meet, are meeting, or have just met knows everything that has ever been posted about us on Google and other omniscient search engines. With a few clicks, all the information collected about us can become available to colleagues, friends, family members, potential employers, or romantic partners. As a result, we also need to ensure that there is a good enough fit between the information that is constantly accumulating about us and available to all at the terminal, and the self we perform in face-to-face interaction. In such conditions, the boundary between public and private realms collapses, and we lose control of both. As Rushkoff notes,

> Today the new permanence of our most casual interactions … turns every transient thought or act into an indelible public recording. Our resumés are no longer distinct from our dating histories … The importance of any given moment is dependent solely on who has found it and what they use it for … Our recorded past then competes with our experienced present for dominance over the moment …[27]

In a pre-terminal age, an individual interacting face-to-face could easily figure out with a reasonable degree of accuracy how many people were present, who they were, and what they knew about him or her. Today, we must assume that those we meet know more—and very differently—about us than we do or than was ever possible. To problematize the situation, we are unaware of the content of all this constantly updated information circulating about us, of the identity of those who produce and search it, their motivations for doing so, and how they're using this information.[28] "Software algorithms are making decisions for organizations about who to deal with and how to deal with them," writes Beer. They are being used to "allocate different levels of service to different users on an increasing automated basis." They shape life-chances, and with decreasing human discretion.[29] As Christl reports in his extensive analysis of corporate surveillance in everyday life,

> Pervasive digital tracking and profiling, in combination with personalization and testing, are not only used to monitor, but also to systematically influence people's behavior. Companies are also increasingly using behavioral data about everyday life situations to make both trivial and consequential automated decisions about people, which may lead to cumulative disadvantages for and discrimination against groups of individuals, and may reinforce or even worsen existing inequalities. These developments affect everyone, whether as individuals or as members of groups—memberships of which one often remains unaware—and, ultimately, the dynamics of society at large.[30]

Our constant activity at the terminal not only produces potentially discreditable information about us, but as trillions of tweets reveal, anybody can now publicly express to countless others anything about us s/he feels like at any particular moment. As Keen notes, "all it takes is a camcorder and a Skype account to actually destroy somebody's life."[31] As the nightly news routinely remind us, other forms of attack at the terminal victimize with equal malice ordinary citizens, state institutions, politicians, and corporations. Having remotely paralyzed and seized terminals, anonymous entities can then copy, steal, corrupt, release, or erase important information stored in them. They can also usurp the owner's identity and ruin his and her reputation. Hence, while we *must* use the terminal to accomplish a growing number of activities, we are the constant potential victims of such devastating attacks. Quickly, anonymously, randomly, and publicly. Senator Anthony Wiener's sexually explicit uploaded photos, General David Petraeus's amorous e-mails, president Trump's tweets, Hillary Clinton's controversial e-mails, and countless others amply demonstrate that these breaches of privacy are astoundingly costly. In light of the current investigation of Russian (cyber-) interference in the 2016 American elections, it is easy to see how the weaponization of private information—and its spectacle—can erode democratic processes and institutions, or obliterate the belief that they are indeed working as intended. At a more micro-level, one cannot help but wonder how living in a state of 'mutually assured humiliation' shapes the spirit of our encounters with others and the relationships we develop with them.[32]

Emoti-con

Until recently, Facebook offered only four options users could select to express their reactions to information they saw at the terminal.[33] Today, if we want to react to a post we've just seen on Facebook, we can select between six emojis, most of which evoke basic and potentially powerful emotions: like, love, amused, surprised, sad, and angry. Interestingly, while the two unambiguously positive emotions (like and love) are represented by the thumb-up and heart icons, respectively, the other four ambiguous or frankly negative emotions are represented by facial features. When we click on those emojis—but also when we fail to do so—we transmit crude emotional signals on how we *feel* about different types of information. As Parisier succinctly put it, "On Google, you are what you click. On Facebook, you are what you share."[34]

We also transmit our reactions through—typically—short comments. We transmit those voluntarily to our 'friends,' but also involuntarily to political, economic, and other entities. Seduced by the cathartic license for self-expression, we might be too distracted to remember that the emotional signals (or silences) we transmit in response to different sorts of information we see at the terminal reveal a great deal about us. They reveal of course what we prefer and 'like,' but also our vulnerabilities and aversions; what outrages, saddens, and disgusts us; what stirs our contempt, and what incites our scorn.

Andrejevic documents that increasing resources are now being invested in data-mining these affective 'click signals' and in performing 'sentiment analysis'.[35] This information will then allow various organizations to not only predict this affective charge, but also to mobilize it, to modulate it, and to attach it to the personalized target *du jour*. That is, to manipulate it. As Pariser notes, "'persuasion profiling' suggests that the kinds of arguments you respond to are highly transferrable from one domain to another."[36] For example, if I click "like" or "share" a certain type of information, I will now increasingly become exposed to other information that—algorithms suggest—I will probably like as well. In other words, the terminal can attach an emotion that I revealed by clicking, onto other domains—food I'd likely enjoy, places where I'd likely want to spend my vacation, books I'd probably like to read, people I'd likely want to meet, movies I'd likely watch, and political causes I'd likely contribute to.

Such information is of course important for organizations interested in mobilizing the flows of affective capitalism. Relentlessly and remotely probing increasingly deeper recesses of subjective experience, this 'political economy of interiority' values especially those 'indicators of authenticity' that we transmit spontaneously. As Ball suggests, those include "emotionality, vulnerability, corporeality, and personal flaws."[37] With the right algorithm, those scattered electronic signals we spontaneously transmit about how we feel—rather than what we think—about a great variety of issues can be easily and quickly assembled into an Achilles' heel that can be strategically poked. As Andrejevic notes, these emotional charges circulate on a plane that is distinct from the one that typically informed the contest between 'factual claims.' They "have the uncanny persistence of 'affective facts': they persist and even thrive on the debunking of the empirical claim to which they are attached."[38] For Rosa also,

It is no longer (if it ever was) the power of the best argument that sets policy, but the power of grudges, of visceral sentiments, of suggestive images and metaphors ... Opinion polls do not reflect a process of deliberation during which arguments could be formulated, discussed, weighed, and tested. On the contrary, they reflect visceral reactions that are largely or even completely immune against the power of the best arguments. Words and even arguments ... have become too slow for the speed of late modern society.[39]

Paradoxically perhaps, in spite of the very mathematical and logical programs that power the terminal, social organizations who/that want to sell us products or ideas know full well that *affective attention* is a most valuable resource in the age of distraction, and exploit it accordingly. And as Facebook's infamous experiment on nearly 700,000 unsuspecting users reveals, the terminal can be used to activate (negative, in this case) emotions among unaware individuals, who then rapidly contaminate others in their networks.[40] The political implications of this ability to manipulate emotions and orchestrate their contagion, amplification, and targeting are far-reaching, especially in the present global climate of fear, polarization, and disruption. Emotional infections that quickly spread through terminal connectivity can give rise to what Bauman calls the "swarm" mentality.[41] Discussing different scenarios of the electronic arms race, Sam Anderson, a designer at the University of Massachusetts Amherst, reminds us that "Twitter's character inhibits nuance, which increases reaction and response."[42] With instant communication and the readily available means of interpersonal violence and intercontinental destruction, such dynamics can be fatal. And while we are fervently expressing our raw and 'authentic' emotions to whomever wants to hear, the digital apparatus is, to quote Andrejevic, "assembling the most comprehensive system of mass monitoring in human history."[43]

Click here to submit

We should not only be concerned by the coercive transparency we must submit to at the terminal but also by the complete asymmetry in transparency.[44] When we willingly trade our privacy for convenience, we acquiesce to a certain *position* in our relationship to the terminal, to the organizations that rely on and require it, and ultimately to ourselves. When we neither control access to our private information nor protect it from intrusion, our autonomy and dignity as free individuals are undermined. This is partly why "the parliamentary assembly of the Council of Europe considers that mass-surveillance is a fundamental threat to human rights."[45] On their end, those who collect and analyze this private information are more likely to perceive users in dehumanized ways as well. As Lynch notes,

A government that sees its citizens' private information as subject to tracking and collection has implicitly adopted a stance toward those citizens inconsistent with the respect due to their inherent dignity as autonomous individuals. It has begun to see them not as persons but as objects to be understood and controlled. That attitude is inconsistent with the demands of democracy itself.[46]

For Zuboff also, a "formal indifference is evident in the aggressiveness with which Google pursues its interests in extracting signals of individual subjectivities."[47] And even if we do not own a Twitter, Facebook, Snapchat, or other similar accounts, and even if we never communicate our emotional reactions at the terminal, millions of other individuals 'just like us' do, in the myriad interactions where they 'connect' and transmit this information about themselves. With the appropriate analytical power, it becomes rather easy to figure out with increasing precision where the 'anger points' and other emotional nerves of entire categories of citizens are located.

Confirm you're not a robot

"Are you human?" a sign-in terminal screen asks. "Please confirm you're not a robot," demands another. Ironically, terminals now require that *I* prove my humanity by copying an alphanumeric code that appears on the screen. If I cannot (or refuse to) do so, they will prevent me from proceeding.

"You've been disconnected." In other instances, we find ourselves summarily expelled from a 'secure' website because we've been 'inactive' for too long. Terminal technologies are not only becoming more efficient at recording, storing, sharing, and updating torrential flows of information, they can also analyze it, make their own decisions, and—more alarmingly—act on them; in real time. Take for example the terminal activating my home security system. If, upon entering, I fail to press the correct sequence of numbers on its keypad within a certain time lapse and 'disarm,' it will activate a deafening siren and immediately transmit information to surveillance personnel located far away. Those individuals will then call me to decide if my home security is indeed compromised or if it's a false alarm. Here, the wrong information I entered at the terminal tripped it to initiate a pre-set sequence of responses, including especially connecting with human beings. While they use sophisticated surveillance technologies (one hopes), those individuals are the final arbiters of the situation.

The bank versateller is another familiar example of a public terminal that has been programed to analyze information, make decisions, and act on them. Thus after I have entered a code and asked for money, the terminal evaluates my balance, decides whether it can disburse the sum I want or not, and proceeds accordingly. In this scenario, human beings who might override terminal decisions are no longer present. Situations like these are becoming increasingly frequent:

> Instead of librarians to check out your book for you, a machine will do it better; instead of clerks to ring out your groceries for you, a self-checkout

will do it better; instead of a real live DJ on the radio, an electronic one will do the job better; instead of a policeman to write you a traffic ticket, a camera (connected to a computer) will do it better.[48]

Facing such a rapid transfer of decision-making power to the terminal, we should examine what kinds of human-machine relationship such transfer normalizes, what kinds of self-reflection it prompts in users, and what it suggests about human autonomy in hypermodern times.

Alas, there is worse. Attempting to understand the consequences of this obliteration of privacy, Bauman and Lyon discuss the increasing merging of technological devices designed for geo-location, remote surveillance, focusing, and targeting—whether it is an enemy combatant or a consumer; or as they suggest, 'target or waste.'[49] As they point out, in the military sphere, the vast distancing between executioners and targets enabled by terminal devices raises important and rather urgent questions about moral responsibility when faceless and anonymous agents remotely unleash violence and destruction upon faceless and anonymous others continents away. The use of drones and other devices of remote targeting and destruction is especially instructive in this respect. At the military terminal, the same gestures can produce outcomes as harmless as remotely piloting surveillance devices across a defined territory, or as catastrophic as launching a 'globocide.' And as important and urgent as those questions obviously are, and as horrifying as the consequences can be when no one is held (or even feels) accountable, recent technological advances in terminal technologies suggest an even greater danger.

In the examples of the static home security or the versateller, terminals are programed to respond in pre-set ways to the information we provide it. Further along the continuum, we find 'programed autonomy'—the ability of terminals devices to *autonomously* collect, process, and integrate vast amounts of information as they move in their environments, make decisions, and execute them. The most disturbing version of this capacity was the subject of a statement presented on July 28, 2015, at the opening of the International Joint Conference on Artificial Intelligence in Buenos Aires. Officially submitted by Stephen Hawking, Steve Wozniak, and an impressive list of technology and science leaders, the statement strongly warned against the development of 'automated killing machines.' Those are essentially intelligent armed robots that will search, locate, and destroy their targets. Programmed by humans, they will execute (people? their mission?) with more speed, power, efficiency, and determination than people will ever muster. Without passion, prejudice, or weakness.

Attending the trial of Nazi war criminal Eichmann in Jerusalem, philosopher Hannah Arendt coined the concept of 'banality of evil' to capture how horrendous acts could be orchestrated and perpetrated by ordinary bureaucrats whose 'stupidity was wholly unexceptional,' and whose main line of defense was that they were 'just following orders.' As many Holocaust stories remind us, however, some would-be perpetrators of horrible crimes could also be tricked, reached, implored, persuaded to show mercy, and to help their 'targets' escape. Such life-saving scenarios cannot, as far as I know, be encoded in a terminal software. Terminals do not follow orders. Programmed by algorithmic "drone vision,"[50] they enact code lines, information. Whether it is about incoming missiles or escaping humans, about a terrorist planning an attack or an individual applying for a life insurance, the terminal interprets everything as information and responds accordingly. Considering the scope, duration, and severity of technological catastrophes, it does not seem unreasonably neurotic to anticipate that, at some point, terminals will most probably escape our control.

Auto–update

> A robot may not injure a human being or, through inaction, allow a human being to come to harm. A robot must obey the orders given it by human beings except where such orders would conflict with the First Law. A robot must protect its own existence as long as such protection does not conflict with the First or Second Laws.[51]

As the famous quote from Asimov's novel *I Robot* implies, we assume that humans are still in the control booth and that they program the terminal's autonomy. But that too is rapidly changing. With the rise of the 'Internet of Things' and other technological leaps, the terminals will be increasingly able to act without human intervention or programming.[52] As Dator et al. warn:

> With the advent of machine learning and bioengineering we may see the mutations and transformations of communication technologies occurring from within the technology itself without the necessity for human agency to unleash, or even guide, these mutative potentialities. Humans may in many ways, no longer be primarily in the driver's seat. As a result we may see the technologies themselves taking on a much more profound role in the shaping of society in the futures beyond the capacity of human agency, which has already been shaped by the tools that make and remake us as humans.[53]

In other words, terminals will soon be able to develop the intelligence necessary to autonomously control their own evolution, and hence, ours. When that time comes, all bets are off.

Notes

1 Google CEO Eric Schmidt, quoted in Rainie and Wellman (2012), 18.
2 Zuboff (2015), 75.
3 Mayer-Schönberger (2009), 7.
4 Lynch (2016), 155.
5 Rainie and Wellman (2012); Lynch (2016), 155.

6 Van Brakel, Moliner, and Clavell (2015), 325.
7 Ragnedda (2011), 181. I have corrected for translation error in the original in English.
8 Quoted in Keen (2012), 76.
9 Fuchs (2017), 205.
10 Ragnedda (2012), 47.
11 Turkle (2011).
12 Turkle (2011), 259.
13 Acquisiti (2011).
14 Marx (2007).
15 Ball (2009), 647.
16 Ragnedda (2011), 187.
17 Levy (2011).
18 Bauman and Lyon (2013), 23.
19 Pariser (2011), 239–240.
20 Fuchs (2017), 343.
21 Ball (2009), 650.
22 Lynch (2016), 107.
23 Ball (2009), 644.
24 Ball (2009), 650.
25 Christl (2017).
26 Dubey (2001).
27 Rushkoff (2013), 156–157.
28 Pariser (2011), 218.
29 Beer (2009), 990.
30 Christl (2017), 84.
31 Keen (2012).
32 Rainie and Wellman (2012).
33 The other choices are "Comment," "Share," or just remain silent.
34 Pariser (2011), 114.
35 Andrejevic (2013), 45.
36 Pariser (2011), 120.
37 Ball (2009), 646.
38 Andrejevic (2013), 60.
39 Rosa (2012), 79.
40 Kramer, Guillory, and Hancock (2014); see also Goel (2014).
41 Bauman (2007), 76.
42 Rainie, Anderson, and Albright (2017), 17.
43 Andrejevic (2013), 60.
44 Andrejevic (2007), 7.
45 Omtzigt (2015), 324.
46 Ibid.
47 Zuboff (2015), 79.
48 Ebert (2011), 162.
49 Bauman and Lyon (2013), 23.
50 Greene (2015).
51 Asimov (2008).
52 The Internet of Things refers to new and often miniaturized technological devices that will make our private and public environments increasingly "intelligent." They will, for example, be able to locate us, sense our moods, anticipate what we are about to do, and react accordingly.
53 Dator, Sweeney, and Yee (2015), 109.

References

Acquisiti, Alessandro. 2011. "Les Comportements de Vie Privée Face au Commerce Éléctronique." *Réseaux* 167: 107–130.

Andrejevic, Mark. 2007. *iSpy: Surveillance and Power in the Interactive Era.* Lawrence, KS: University Press of Kansas.

Andrejevic, Mark. 2013. *Infoglut: How Too Much Information Is Changing the Way We Think and Know.* New York: Routledge.

Asimov, Isaac. 2008. *I, Robot.* New York: Spectra.

Ball, Kirstie. 2009. "Exposure: Exploring the Subject of Surveillance." *Information, Communication and Society* 12(5): 639–657.

Bauman, Zygmunt and David Lyon. 2013. *Liquid Surveillance.* Cambridge, UK: Polity.

Beer, David. 2009. "Power through the Algorithm? Participatory Web Cultures and the *Technological Unconscious*." *New Media & Society* 11(6): 985–1002.

Dator, James A., John A. Sweeney, and Aubrey M. Yee. 2015. *Mutative Media: Communication Technologies and Power Relations in the Past, Present, and Futures.* Lecture Notes in Social Networks. Switzerland: Springer International Publishing.

Dubey, Gérard. 2001. *Le Lien Social à l'ère du Virtuel.* Paris: Presses Universitaires de France.

Ebert, John David. 2011. *The New Media Invasion: Digital Technologies and the World They Unmake.* Jefferson, NC: McFarlane.

Fuchs, Christian. 2017. *Social Media: A Critical Introduction.* Los Angeles: Sage.

Greene, Daniel. 2015. "Drone Vision." *Surveillance & Society* 13(2): 233–249.

Keen, Andrew. 2012. *Digital Vertigo: How Today's Online Social Revolution is Dividing, Diminishing, and Disorienting Us.* New York: St. Martin Griffin, 53.

Kramer, Adam, D., Jamie E. Guillory, and Jeffrey T. Hancock. 2014. "Experimental Evidence of Massive-Scale Emotional Contagion through Social Networks." *Proceedings of the National Academy of Sciences* 111(24): 8788–8790.

Levy, Matthew. 2011. "A Notion of Faces, Not Laws: Facebook as Ideological Platform." *Fast Capitalism* 8(1). Retrieved June 11, 2015. www.uta.edu/huma/agger/fastcapitalism/8_1/levy8_1.html.

Lynch, Michael Patrick. 2016. *The Internet of Us: Knowing More and Understanding Less in the Age of Big Data.* New York: Liveright.

Marx, Gary T. 2007. "Soft Surveillance: The Growth of Mandatory Voluteerism in Collecting Personal Information." pp. 37–56 in *Surveillance and Security: Technological Politics and Power in Everyday Life*, T. Monahan (ed.). London: Routledge.

Mayer-Schonberger, Viktor. 2011. *Delete: The Virtue of Forgetting in the Digital Age.* Princeton, NJ: Princeton University Press.

Omtzigt, Pieter. 2015. "Mass Surveillance." Parliamentary Assembly, Council of Europe, January 26, 2015. Quoted in Rosamunde Van Brakel, Liliana A. Moliner, and Gemma G. Clavell. "Surveillance: Ambiguities and Asymmetries." *Surveillance & Society* 13(3/4): 324–325.

Pariser, Eli. 2011. *The Filter Bubble: How the New Personalized Web is Changing What We Read and How We Think.* New York: Penguin.

Ragnedda, Massimo. 2011. "Social Control and Surveillance in the Society of Consumers." *International Journal of Sociology and Anthropology* 3(6): 180–188.

Rainie, Lee and Barry Wellman. 2012. *Networked: The New Social Operating System.* Cambridge, MA: MIT Press.

Rainie, Lee, Janna Anderson, and Jonathan Albright. 2017. "The Future of Free Speech, Trolls, Anonymity, and Fake News Online." Pew Research Center, March 2017. Available at: www.pewinternet.org/2017/03/29/the-future-of-free-speech-trolls-anonymity-and-fake-news-online/. Downloaded June 9, 2017.

Rosa, Hartmut. 2012. *Aliénation et Accélération: Vers une Théorie Critique de la Modernité Tardive*. Paris: La Découverte.

Rushkoff, Douglas. 2013. *Present Shock: When Everything Happens Now*. New York: Penguin.

Turkle, Sherry. 2011. *Alone Together: Why We Demand More of Technology and Less of Each Other*. New York: Basic Books.

Van Brakel, Rosamunde, Liliana A. Moliner, and Gemma G. Clavell. 2015. "Surveillance: Ambiguities and Asymmetries." *Surveillance & Society* 13(3/4): 324–326.

Zuboff, Shoshana. 2015. "Big Other: Surveillance Capitalism and the Prospects of an Information Civilization." *Journal of Information Technology* (30): 75–89.

8   Disable

> For the first time in history, a society has felt its economic survival demands a kind of controlled regression, a culture that promotes puerility rather than maturation.[1]

According to the dictionary, to infantilize is "to keep in or reduce to an infantile state; to treat or regard as infantile or immature; to treat or condescend to as if still a young child." In this chapter, I suggest that, in concert, the five terminal default settings I have discussed in the previous chapters normalize and reward infantile dispositions among users. At the same time, as the quote by Barber above suggests, this technologically-induced infantilization articulates and accelerates a similar trend that has been documented in a variety of hypermodern social institutions. I first discuss the problem surrounding the idea of infantilization at a societal level, review scholarship on this trend, and then re-visit those features of terminal interactions that normalize and reward infantile dispositions in adult users.

Select parental control settings

"Men dress up like children and children dress up like superheroes," remarks Greenberg upon entering a party in a Los Angeles home.[2] With this simple remark, the (anti-)hero of the eponymous movie, played by Ben Stiller, expresses a relatively recent topic of scholarship. For example, in his book *Consumed*, Benjamin Barber discusses an 'infantilist ethos' that seems to increasingly characterize contemporary culture and politics.[3] Referring to the common-sense assumptions we (un)consciously embrace and everyday practices we (un)consciously perform as we participate in various social institutions, this ethos unreflectively favors easy over hard, simple over complex, and fast over slow. "Americans can no longer think of one another as grown-ups," writes Konigsberg.[4] And while we might find this new ethos trivial and unworthy of academic attention, Barber reminds us that "infantilism's preference for simple, easy, and fast gives it an affinity for certain political forms over others."[5] And typically not intelligent ones.

At first glance, it seems that what is considered 'acting one's age' is quite relative. After all, the ancient Israelites considered a thirteen-year old boy to be a man who was fully responsible for his actions,[6] and Mohandas Gandhi married at thirteen. In colonial America, girls as young as seven were considered fit for marriage, and today, in a number of countries, they are married at that age. Historical and anthropological research never cease to provide us with intriguing reminders that in many time periods and societies, individuals we today consider young were seen as adults, and people we today categorize as middle-aged were considered old. On the other hand, if the organization of life stages is historically and culturally relative,[7] in most societies, members typically distinguish between behaviors deemed appropriate for different stages of the life-cycle—however they slice it—and typically notice those that are not. Thus, for example, while the successive stages of the life-cycle are organized quite differently in our society than they were around 57 AD in the Middle East, 1 Corinthians (13:11) is still clear about important distinctions between them: "When I was a child, I talked like a child, I thought like a child, I reasoned like a child. When I became a man, I put childish ways behind me." Accordingly, I will suggest that an infantile individual is a person who fails to enact the cognitive, affective, and interpersonal qualities that are considered appropriate to his or her stage in the life-cycle, and who instead enacts those that s/he acquired in a previous stage of development. The infantile individual is a regressive one.

Of course, spontaneous and intermittent childlike behaviors in adults are far from being inherently problematic. As Maslow suggested, such behaviors can—in context—be therapeutic, endearing, facilitating interactions between adults, and between adults and children.[8] In addition, children's behaviors include many positive traits such as curiosity, openness to experience, and intuitive sensitivity to others—traits that are valuable among adults as well. But spontaneously occurring and intermittent childlike behaviors among adults are different from regressive trends that are systematically encouraged by the key social institutions in which they participate. And when the underlying assumptions and everyday practices that guide such participation fail to promote adult psychosocial aptitudes in adults, they infantilize individuals, they disempower and *disable* them. They normalize regressive dispositions that are otherwise well-adapted to the needs of a hypermodern 'affective capitalism.'[9]

For Blatterer, young and not so young people find the traditional criteria of adulthood (marriage, work, parenting, and independent living) uninspiring and poorly adapted to contemporary economic and cultural conditions.[10] When these obsolete criteria are critically examined in light of extent conditions, the seemingly pandemic 'refusal to grow up' might express not a generational pathology, but an adaptive and much-needed innovation. As Zerzan notes,

> Not only, as a foundation of modern life, does the encroaching high-tech principle render us all daily more dependent; the institutions of society—and media is only the most glaring example—are themselves infantile and

infantilizing. Who would legitimately feel anything but the need to 'regress' in the opposite direction of such a non-future?[11]

Accordingly, Blatterer proposes that new criteria of adulthood, such as risk-taking, commitment to short-term projects, and flexibility across contexts, might be more relevant to assess adulthood in the accelerating present. However, while these criteria seem indeed invaluable to help navigate turbulent hypermodern currents, and might indeed evidence adaptability, they are individualistic. They do not seem motivated by the basic drive to connect with others in order to develop with them a mutually nurturing and co-evolving relationship, which is ultimately the basic drive of a healthy social and psychological existence, and of life itself. In other words, if—like many other areas of study—contemporary scholarship on adulthood remains prisoner of obsolete criteria, we must still acknowledge that leading psychological theories as well as major spiritual systems rooted in vastly different cultures have consistently located maturity in qualities that convey a decidedly *social* rather than *individualistic* orientation. Empathy, compassion, altruism, patience, care, love, responsibility, trustworthiness, dependability, humility, honesty, loyalty, self-sacrifice, forgiveness, and commitment to a project greater than oneself all evoke (adult) other-directed dispositions and behaviors rather than individualistic and self-serving proclivities one performs for no one in particular.[12] Sadly, Jackson writes, "a quarter of Americans report having no close confidantes, double the number who reported such a degree of isolation in 1985."[13] Similarly, in a recent *New York Times* editorial, Khullar reports that the percentage of Americans who say they feel lonely has recently doubled to 40 percent. As he notes, such a condition is literally killing many of those so afflicted.[14]

Reduce size

Blatterer proposes to resolve the conundrum of the culturally relative criteria of adulthood by affirming that "recognition of individuals as full members of society … is the meaningful constant of adulthood."[15] However, it seems that—especially in complex and rapidly changing societies—the nature of this recognition, its sources, the authority it bestows, its durability, and transferability across contexts are unclear. For example, an individual may be treated—and feel like—an adult at home, but routinely face infantilization at work. Or she might be treated as an adult at work, but infantilized as a patient, a parishioner, a consumer, or a voter.

During his first trip to America in 1946, French anthropologist Claude Lévi-Strauss commented on the distinctively (and often endearing) infantile traits of American culture.[16] Contemporary scholars note, however, that such traits have become noticeably both less charming and more widespread. In the sphere of production, for example, Hebdige's remarks about the working conditions enforced on Disneyland employees are quite evocative:

Infantilization—the rendering mute, dependent, powerless—of large sections of the adult population is one result of a process whereby employees … bludgeoned into submission by downsizing, deskilling and temporary contracts—are made to audition for their jobs on a daily basis, are expected, on pain of summary dismissal, to defer automatically to all 'superiors,' to stay 'in role,' 'on script' and 'in view'—subject to surveillance by company-appointed supervisors for however long the shift lasts at the work-place.[17]

Analyzing the effects of terminal-based monitoring in the workplace, Gary Marx also concludes that:

workers may feel they are being treated like children … and interpret the workplace to be saying "We don't trust you. We expect you to behave irresponsibly, to take advantage, and to screw up unless we remove all temptation and prevent you from doing so or trick or force you to do otherwise."[18]

Infantilizing trends in the workplace are of course not limited to Disneyland or the US. For example, Max Pagès finds that the French multinational corporation he researched achieved control of workers through voluntary "massive collective regression."[19] Gustavsson finds similar infantilizing trends in Sweden[20] and Eriksen detects them in Norway.[21]

Belk analyzes the infantilization of Las Vegas tourists[22] and Mark Derry detects it in architectural trends such as Disney's planned communities:

In an America racked by social change and economic inequity, where community and civility are fast unraveling, Disney promises to time-warp an anxious middle-class to a revisionist past (or is it a neotraditional future?) where our corporate parents unburden us of our rights and responsibilities as citizens so that we may folic in secret forts and hop-scotch on the streets like the inner children we've always been at heart.[23]

Hebdige describes the infantile expressions on display in contemporary art galleries,[24] and Berman exposes similar 'dumbing down' tendencies in the educational institution, in literature, in action movies, in TV programs, in sound bites from presidential candidates, and in other popular media texts.[25]

The link between capitalism and infantilizing mass media is hardly new and has been the topic of a voluminous scholarship. Jappe, for example reminds us that for Debord and Adorno

the infantilization of the spectator is no mere side-effect of the spectacle and the culture industry, but the embodiment of their anti-emancipatory goals: for Adorno, the ideal of the culture industry is to reduce adults to "the level of twelve-year-olds;" for Debord, "the need to imitate that the consumer experiences is a truly infantile need."[26]

As conservative journalist George Will also concludes,

> in an increasingly infantilized society, whose moral philosophy is reducible to a celebration of 'choice', adults are decreasingly distinguishable from children in their absorption in entertainments and the kinds of entertainments they are absorbed in—video games, computer games, hand-held games, movies on their computers and so on. This is progress: more sophisticated delivery of stupidity.[27]

Empirically demonstrating infantilizing trends across the main types of mass media, Bernardini also detects them in the very nature of contemporary consumption:

> It is easily suggestible, tends to want objects that have no utilitarian purpose; is driven by individualistic, irrational and almost exclusively playful desire; does not take into account the needs of others and does not present a substantial diversification in tastes.[28]

For Lipovetsky, also, the hypermodern 'turbo-consumption' is an example par excellence of this trend:

> If old people want to look like young people, the young refuse to grow up. While the market for regressive consumption develops, the refusal to grow up starts increasingly earlier, as young adults seem to want to live in the eternal prolongation of their childhood or adolescence … Phillipe Muray … has not hesitated to see in our "universalized nursery" a sign of the death of historical human beings, a "crucial moment in the mutation of a humanity" that has suddenly become reinfantilized, babyphilic, undifferentiated, transgressive, and monstrous.[29]

Martynova and Glukhov's research also detects this infantilization in new linguistic patterns in both the US and Russia,[30] and Guzman reports it in Spain.[31] Beyond those trends in major social institutions,[32] hypermodern theorist Barus-Michel also locates them in the very "symbolic system that encodes and structures the representations of hypermodernity." Reduced to the simplest expression (the information flash) so as to communicate short and dramatic information, this symbolic system is articulated in a language that is becoming "poorer, binary, and similar to computer language." Promoting an infantile morality, this language "does not allow thinking or sense-making, but aims to shock."[33]

Infantilizing trends are also audible in what Frank Furedi calls a "therapy culture" that spreads well beyond the walls of the psychologist's office.[34] As he warns, such a culture endorses a view of adults as vulnerable, weak, and fragile subjects whose troubles qualify them for a 'permanent suspension of moral sense,' and whose successful prognosis requires continuous dependence on a therapist's expert knowledge so as to overcome the obstacles they stumble upon in the trenches of everyday life. In his opinion, to insist that unfortunate childhood experiences so powerfully shape adult life absolves grown-ups from adult responsibilities, erodes their trust in their own experiences and insights, weakens their social networks, and fundamentally shapes how they relate to others. By "psychologizing" a growing number of human behaviors, therapeutic culture ensures both this permanent sense of vulnerability and this dependence.[35] Of course, therapy is important and can have many benefits. After all, the stories we tell about who we are and what ails us matter for how we understand ourselves and what we feel capable of doing. Stories can inspire regression or evolution, but regression is always easier, especially when it is rewarded.

Minimize

While scholars such as Côté[36] and Cross[37] remind us that infantilizing trends in our society began well before Web 3.0, the five previous chapters suggest that several features of the terminal mode of interaction both normalize and amplify them. In "Sync," I proposed that the default setting of terminal *interactivity* invites constant dependence, a simplified engagement with reality, a presentist orientation, de-realization, degraded cognitive functions, and a decline in the sense of agency. In "Personalize," I offered that the terminal default setting of *customization* re-orients the user's experience of self as central, omnipotent, and sufficient. In "Validate," I argued that the terminal default setting or imperative of *visibility* deforms the mechanisms of social recognition, incites self-inflated exhibitionism, and rewards performances of the self that are typically frowned upon in adult face-to-face interactions.[38] In "Ignore," I indicated that the terminal default setting for *connectivity* deteriorates users' abilities to role-take, to perform face-work, and to manage the need for adult social recognition. In "Submit," I concluded that the terminal default setting for constant *surveillance* induces a submissive attitude and robs users' sense of privacy, integrity, and autonomy. Indeed, the aggressive violation of users' privacy rights already announces that they are not worthy of this fundamental adult right.

Incited by the terminal mode of interactivity, these infantile dispositions are of course interrelated and mutually reinforcing. In fact, our interactions with the terminal can be so pleasurable—and for many, addictive—precisely because, beyond the high-tech language, they normalize and reward infantile cravings. They shrink our horizon to the urgent present and locate the center in the self. They reduce our interactions to simple messages and limit our participation to obedient information-management. They instantly validate whatever we are doing and absolve us of adult responsibilities. The infantilization incited by terminal interactions is purposeful and will intensify. As former Google marketing manager Tristan Harris explains, companies that compete to find the quickest and cheapest program for 'brain-hacking' quickly "race to the bottom of the brain stem."[39] Alarmingly, however, the socially-engineered infantilist regression enforced in everyday institutions and the technologically 'induced puerility'[40] prompted by terminal interactions are rapidly deteriorating key adult capacities at the very moment when we need them most.

Notes

1 Barber (2008), 111.
2 Baumbach (2010).
3 Barber (2008).
4 Quoted in Daly and Wice (1995), 113. See also Calcutt (2000).
5 Barber (2008), 107.
6 Hence, the concept, ritual, or life-stage associated with the Jewish *bar-mitzvah*.
7 Aries (1965).
8 Maslow (1962).
9 Andrejevic (2013).
10 Blatterer (2007).
11 Zerzan (2006).
12 While there exist cultures where members associate adulthood with dispositions such as cruelty, manipulation, stubbornness, domination, isolation, dishonesty, and a paranoid worldview, these seem to be the exception rather than the rule. Although typically considered negative, they are still oriented towards another, albeit in a pathological way.
13 Jackson (2009), 59–60.
14 Khullar (2016).
15 Blatterer (2007).
16 Levi-Strauss (1946).
17 Hebdige (2003), 161.
18 Marx (2016), 194.
19 Pagès (2005), 230.
20 Gustavsson (2005).
21 Eriksen (2001).
22 Belk (2000).
23 Dery (1999), 178–179.
24 Hebdige (2003).
25 Berman (2006), 27; see also Boghosian (2003).
26 Jappe (1999).
27 Quoted in Dator et al. (2015), 129.
28 Bernardini (2014).
29 Lipovetsky (2006), 65.
30 Martynnova and Glukhov (2015).
31 Guzman (2015).
32 Berman (2000), 44–59.
33 Barus-Michel (2005), 246–247.
34 Although an increasing number of people now access the terminal to also receive therapy.
35 Furedi (2004).
36 Côté (2000).
37 Cross (2008).
38 These include public pronouncements of one's accomplishments, inflated claims, intense emotional reactions, provocations, overt and public requests for attention, and inappropriate intimacy, for example.
39 Cooper (2017).
40 Barber (2008), 3.

References

Aries, Phillipe. 1965. *Centuries of Childhood: A Social History of Family Life*. New York: Vintage.

Barber, Benjamin. 2008. *Consumed: How Markets Corrupt Children, Infantilize Adults, and Swallow Citizens Whole*. New York: W. W. Norton & Co.

Barus-Michel, Jacqueline. 2005. "L'Hypermodernité, Dépassement ou Perversion de la Modernité?" pp. 246–247 in *L'Individu Hypermoderne*, Nicole Aubert (ed.). Toulouse: Érès.

Baumbach, Noah. 2010. *Greenberg*, movie. Los Angeles: Focus Features.

Belk, Russel. 2000. "May the Farce be With You: On Las Vegas and Consumer Infantilization." *Consumption, Markets and Culture* 4(2): 101–124.

Berman, Morris. 2000. *The Twilight of American Culture*. New York: W. W. Norton & Co.

Berman, Morris. 2006. *Dark Ages America: The Final Phase of Empire*. New York: W. W. Norton & Co.

Bernardini, Jacopo. 2014. "The Infantilization of the Postmodern Adult and the Figure of Kidult." *Postmodern Openings* 5(2): 39–55.

Blatterer, Harry. 2007. "Contemporary Adulthood: Reconceptualizing an Uncontested Category." *Current Sociology* 55: 771–792.

Boghosian, John Arden. 2003. *America's Meltdown: The Lower-Common-Denominator Society*. Westport, CT: Praeger.

Calcutt, Andrew. 2000. *Arrested Development: Pop Culture and the Erosion of Adulthood*. London and New York: Cassell.

Cooper, Anderson. 2017. "What is Brain Hacking? Tech Insiders on Why You Should Care." *60 Minutes*. CBS. June 11. www.cbsnews.com/news/what-is-brain-hacking-tech-insiders-on-why-you-should-care/.

Côté, James. 2000. *Arrested Adulthood: The Changing Nature of Maturity and Identity*. New York: New York University Press.

Cross, Gary. 2008. *Men to Boys: The Making of Modern Immaturity*. New York: Columbia University Press.

Daly, Steven and Nathaniel Wice. 1995. *alt.culture: An A-to-Z Guide to the 90s—Underground, Online, and Over-the-Counter*. New York: Harper-Perennial.

Dator, James A., John A. Sweeney, and Aubrey M. Yee. 2015. *Mutative Media: Communication Technologies and Power Relations in the Past, Present, and Futures*. Lecture Notes in Social Networks. Switzerland: Springer International Publishing.

Dery, Mark. 1999. *The Pyrotechnic Insanitarium: American Culture on the Brink*. New York: Grove Press.

Eriksen, Thomas Hylland. 2001. *The Tranny of the Moment: Fast and Slow Time in the Information Age*. London: Pluto Press.

Furedi, Frank. 2004. *Therapy Culture: Cultivating Vulnerability in an Uncertain Age*. London: Routledge.

Gustavsson, Bengt. 2005. "The Ethics of Managing Corporate Identity." *Journal of Human Values* 11: 9–29.

Guzman, Javier. 2015. "8 de cada 10 Personas son Incapaces de Hacer Discursos de Un Minuto." *El Pais* July 10. http://elpais.com/elpais/2015/07/30/videos/1438279001_736056.htm.

Hebdige, Dick. 2003. "Dis-Gnosis: Disney and the Re-Tooling of Knowledge, Art, Culture, Life, Etc." *Cultural Studies* 17(2): 150–167.

Jackson, Maggie. 2009. *Distracted: The Erosion of Attention and the Coming Dark Age*. New York: Prometheus.

Jappe, Anselm. 1999. "Sic Transit Gloria Artis: 'The End of Art' for Theodor Adorno and Guy Debord." *Substance* 90: 102–128.

Khullar, Dhruv. 2016. "How Social Isolation Is Killing Us." *New York Times*. www.nytimes.com/2016/12/22/upshot/how-social-isolation-is-killing-us.html.

Levi-Strauss, Claude. 1946. "La Technique du Bonheur aux USA." *Age D'Or* 1: 75–83.

Lipovetsky, Gilles. 2006. *Le Bonheur Paradoxal: Essai sur la Société d'Hyperconsommation*. Paris: Gallimard.

Martynnova, Irina A. and Gennady V. Glukhov. 2015. "Exploring the Echoes of Social Changes: Case Study of Language Infantilism." *Mediterranean Journal of Social Sciences* 6(6): 315–322.

Marx, Gary T. 2016. *Windows into the Soul: Surveillance and Society in an Age of High Technology*. University of Chicago Press.

Maslow, Abraham. 1962. *Toward a Psychology of Being*. New York: Van Nostrand.

Pagès, Max. 2005. "Massification, Regression, Violence Dans La Société Contemporaine." pp. 229–238 in *L'Individu Hypermoderne*, Nicole Aubert (ed.). Toulouse: Erès.

Zerzan, John. 2006. "Youth and Regression in an Infantile Society." Retrieved March 30. www.primitivism.com.

9   Save as

"Allô. SNCB?" I ask the person who just picked up the phone.[1]

"Yes," answers the slightly irritated female voice on the other end of the line, "how can I help you?"

"Hi. Your system charged me twice for the same train ticket and I would like to be reimbursed," I answer with a voice that, I hope, projects both decisiveness and expertise.

"Let's see … first you'll have to give me some information." I give her all the details of my purchase that, judging by her silence and the rapid clicking sounds, she is typing into her terminal. After what seems like an inordinately long time, she comes back online. "Ah voilà," she says, "yes, two round-trips Brussels-Paris at 11:15am. December 19."

"Well, you see. It's a computer mistake. I could not logically have purchased two tickets on the same train for the same person," I answer, trying to stay calm.

"But you did! The computer clearly indicates that you did," she accuses, now frankly miffed.

"It's a computer mistake," I insist. "Look, I've been managing transatlantic flights since I'm sixteen years old and I don't have a multiple personality disorder. I would have never made that kind of mistake. Why can't you admit that maybe, just maybe, your computer might be at fault?" I know I'm losing my cool, but I'm beginning to feel the shivers of mounting catharsis.

"Sir, we don't have the technical capacity to reimburse or change your ticket," she announces in a stern voice.

"It's always the same thing," I respond, "the system commits errors, and then no one seems to have the authority to …"

"It's not the *authority*," she interrupts, "it's the *technical capacity*. Do you appreciate the nuance?"

"Oh, but I do. Still, it's kind of a lame excuse. If your system can take my money, it should have the *technical capacity* to return it." Now I know I've lost.

"If you want, I can give you the address of the customer service department. You can write them a letter explaining your case," she must be smirking.

"No, thank you. Bye. Have a nice day."

As I am resigning myself to the loss of nearly 100 euros on account of a computer error that no letter will ever resolve, I am also contemplating a more worrisome new situation where terminals are given more authority than humans about what concerns us, where my lived experience of 40 years traveling across three continents does not measure up to terminal accounts. Ironically, the next day, the news announced that the SNCB website had been hacked, and data on millions of users stolen. Should I feel vindicated? Or worried that the simple replication of a train ticket by the terminal points at much more dreadful developments?

Show profile

Several hypermodernists posit that the current moment is witnessing important sociological and anthropological mutations. At the micro-level, they are discernible in bodies altered by nano-technology,[2] genetic engineering, and performance-enhancing drugs; in minds that are calibrated by mood-stabilizing substances, and in new trends of mental disorders. At the macro level, these mutations are noticeable in acceleration, excess, and the re-organization of all major institutions around the logic of the new digital apparatus. French sociologist Virilio calls it "technological fundamentalism." As he explains,

> fundamentalism in the sense of a monotheism of information. No longer the monotheism of the Written Word, of the Koran, of the Bible, of the New Testament, but a monotheism of information in the widest sense of the term. And this information monotheism has come into being not simply in a totally independent manner but also free from any controversy. It is the outcome of an intelligence without reflection or past. And with information monotheism comes what I think of as the greatest danger of all, the slide into a future without humanity. I believe that violence, and even a kind of "hyper-violence," springs out of technological fundamentalism.[3]

From the neural to the ecological, the mutations unleashed by the digital apparatus present us with increasing risks, and by the time we have wrapped our minds around a specific number of known risks, new and unforeseen ones suddenly appear, interact in complex ways with those we think we understand, and require both immediate attention and more elaborate thinking. However, synced to the terminal, our very attention is increasingly overwhelmed, scattered, and depleted,[4] and our very thinking is becoming compromised. Reflecting on the present and future of the internet, experts are overall not optimistic,[5] and many note that the synergy between the means of terminal interaction, state surveillance, and consumption produces a power that rivals every other known example in history. For obvious reasons, this power must be resisted.

How to do so? There is of course a growing number of hacktivist individuals and organizations, such as Anonymous and Wikileaks, that resist this new power by infiltrating targeted terminals and releasing damaging information about guilty economic, cultural, and political agents. Other organizations, such as the Electronic Frontier Foundation and the American Civil Liberties Union, for example, resist the invasion of our privacy and other corporate misbehaviors by legal means, political campaigns, and other conventional democratic mechanisms.[6] Websites such as the Open Whisper Systems and the Tor Project enable users to surf the Web while remaining anonymous, and still other sites such as AlterNet, Democracy Now! OpenDemocracy, and Indymedia provide alternative and critical sources of information.[7] Discussing the concept of "socialist privacy protection," Fuchs proposes seven political-economic strategies to protect consumers in cyberspace and the information environment:

> (1) the use of data protection legislation; (2) the advancement of an opt-in online advertising; (3) civil society surveillance of Internet companies; (4) digital labour unionism; (5) the establishment and support of alternative platforms; (6) corporate taxation and a participatory media fee; (7) the establishment of an alternative societal context of internet use.[8]

While those organizations and strategies are obviously necessary and valuable, resistance must also take the form of isolated and collective critical interventions at the interpersonal level, as such interventions resist the more subtle subversion of everyday life by the digital apparatus. In other words, while necessary changes must be officially and legally implemented in various social institutions, one should not forget the necessary changes that we the users must implement in our interactions with others, in our orientations, and in our everyday habits.

It seems that the first necessary step to mount resistance at this level is to recognize how we nonchalantly adjust ourselves—our thoughts, perceptions, and orientations—to the terminal logic. And since those adjustments carry over in our face-to-face-encounters, we should exercise this reflective awareness in the latter realm as well, and in the reciprocal influences between the two. Rather than normalizing the new mode of terminal interaction, we should remind ourselves and each other of its strangeness, of the peculiar behaviors and orientations it prompts in us. We should remain alert to those social arrangements that hinder this ability, knowledgeable about their distorting effects, able to discuss them, and willing to counteract them.[9] While by no means sufficient, this awareness can at least help keep the face-to-face channels of communication open, and this affordance will, I believe, help the terminal self confront three major risks. Those pertain to the intrapersonal, the interpersonal, and the societal levels. While I have mentioned those risks in previous chapters, in guise of a conclusion, I re-visit them here and propose various strategies to confront them.

The generalized terminal other

One first risk the terminal self confronts is the rapid degrading of human faculties, such as the dexterous manipulation of concrete objects, perception, memory-formation, information-management, reality-testing, and a sense of agency. By degrading these seemingly isolated individual faculties, terminal interactions also disrupt their integration. In so doing, they impoverish the quality and richness of the terminal self's subjective experience, his and her sense of potentialities, and imagination.

In symbolic interaction theory, we develop a sense of self by taking the role with, and self-reflecting from, another's point of view. Starting with a concrete significant other, this ability evolves to include the point of view of an increasingly abstract and imagined 'generalized other.' This capacity needs not be limited to humans. Arluke and Sanders note that we can extend it to animals,[10] and Irvine adds that some animals can also self-reflect from our points of view.[11] For green symbolic interactionists such as Weigert, we can (and should) also extend this capacity farther (and deeper), and self-reflect from the point of view of a generalized *environmental* other, when we evaluate the ethical dimensions and long-term consequences of our 'transverse interactions' with the natural environment.[12]

But what about a generalized *terminal* other? After all, we don't just utilize our personalized terminal, we *interact* with it, it interacts with us; it is fast becoming our constant interactional partner. It knows more about us than we do, and in ways we cannot fathom. Because it is easier to take the role and self-reflect from the point of another who/that responds—and even anticipates—our intentions, it seems likely that our interactions with the personalized terminal will increase in frequency, centrality, and desirability.

And as terminal intrusions in our everyday life and thoughts become more frequent, its point of view displaces other—human—ones, and disrupts the chorus of inner voices we typically activate when we self-reflect. This new generalized other, and the consciousness it summons, operates according to incongruous interaction criteria and disregards familiar assumptions about what is the self, how it should and can relate to the social world, and how this social world typically responds. For the first time in the history of human consciousness also, this generalized other is encoded by technological exigencies rather than guided by human concerns.

One strategy terminal selves can use to resist this 'brain-hacking' is to re-evaluate their relations to the terminal, to limit their interactions with it to particular places, times, and functions; in other words, to domesticate it more actively. By refusing a 'frictionless' adjustment, this strategic and deliberate use of the terminal can enhance users' ability to resist the deskilling and dumbing down tendencies this adjustment requires. It prompts the cultivation of skills and embodied knowledges that users discard when they rely on terminal shortcuts and apps. It can help ground users in physical space, re-activate their senses, and mend the integration between them. It can better shield them from the violent fragmentation detonated by what Virilio calls the "information bomb,"[13] and better enable them to resist the state of distracted urgency imposed by the regime of perpetual connectivity.[14] As a result, users can better control how they live, at what tempo, and in whose company.

A related risk preying at the intrapersonal level is that what we communicate at the terminal is increasingly granted more authority in defining who we are than what we communicate in face-to-face encounters. If knowledge about the context of a communicative act is essential to interpret that act correctly, any attempt to interpret it out of context will logically be incomplete and incorrect. This is especially the case when the terminal—the context where we act—is radically different from the contexts where others (mis)interpret that act. Paradoxically, however, while the words we transmit at the terminal seem more 'real' than those we communicate face-to-face (after all, they are recorded data), they are in fact less so and must be treated accordingly.

The same obtains for the information we transmit unintentionally by our sheer activity at the terminal. Those signals are assembled to create a digital 'identity,' 'shadow' or profile. And the more frequent our activity at the terminal, the more detailed and distinct this profile becomes. And the more detailed and distinct this digital profile becomes, the more authority it gains as a valid and reliable source of information about who we—and others—think we are. This terminal profile is increasingly used to evaluate us but also to predict our behavior. As Rainie and Anderson note, "prediction possibilities follow us like a pet. The result: As information tool and predictive dynamics are more widely adopted, our lives will be increasingly affected by their inherent conclusions and the narratives they spawn."[15]

As the digital apparatus is becoming increasingly efficient at managing swelling flows of information about us, those embodied experiences or activities that are not digitized (or formatted for the terminal) will become less pertinent, substantial, or credible. Restricted by mindless digital narratives, the terminal self may develop a rather distorted understanding of his or her biographical experiences and the enduring lessons those can teach. As Greenfield elegantly put it,

> The individual networked in this way is no longer the autonomous subject enshrined in liberal theory, not precisely. Our very selfhood is smeared out across a global mesh of nodes and links; all the aspects of our personality we think of as constituting who we are—our tastes, preferences, capabilities, desires—we owe to the fact of our connection with that mesh, and the selves and distant resources to which it binds us.[16]

Absent from the terminal, excluded from our 'profile,' fading from our already compromised memories, disconnected from each other and from a larger biography, these embodied experiences will no longer serve as important sources of knowledge that we can mobilize to question the claimed authenticity of the digital profile, and to challenge the authority it wields in defining who we are.

In addition, while the search engines of the digital apparatus collect information about us for purposes of surveillance and manipulation, we do not have the right to know what information is being collected about us, who has access to it, who is collecting it, what they do with it, and for what purpose. Nor do we have the right to edit it, nor to have access to parallel information about those who wield this power over us. We thus find ourselves unilaterally monitored, powerless, uninformed, and, as Fuchs suggests, exploited:

> Google users are unpaid Google workers who create large parts of Google's value and profits ... Internet users are not consumers or audiences, they are active creators, productive consumers (prosumers), and consumption workers, who create content, social relations, transaction data and attention.[17]

Accordingly, it seems that those who supply this value should have more control over the conditions of its production, commodification, sale, and consumption. And if the right to control the information that circulates about users cannot be granted because of seemingly unresolvable technological difficulties, then, the same level of transparency should be imposed equally on everyone. This demand is neither unrealistic nor utopian. Democracy requires privacy, and freedom entails protection from invasion—be it physical or electronic. While the 'right to disconnect' seems today to be a luxury enjoyed by members of privileged social strata, it should be extended to all citizens.[18] As Eggers put it in his novel *The Circle*,

> We must all have the right to anonymity. Not every human activity can be measured. The ceaseless pursuit of data to quantify the value of any endeavor is catastrophic to true understanding. The barrier between public and private must remain unbreachable ... We must all have the right to disappear.[19]

Until this right is granted, we should also remain alert to and—whenever possible—refuse to comply to those now routine requests for private information we must surrender in order to simply participate in the institutions of everyday life. If that refusal is not possible, then another form of resistance is electronic sabotage—in this case, giving the digital apparatus incorrect information.

Low resolution

The terminal mode of interaction inevitably distorts how individuals relate to each other—the second risk confronting the terminal self. Facing disintegration unleashed by the forces of violent acceleration and excess, lacking grounds and horizon, the terminal self responds through depressed detachment at one extreme and a strident need for recognition at the other. Reduced to a *performance* whose criteria are constantly ratcheted up, this caricatured and harried need for recognition is increasingly frustrated by a society-wide declining ability to role-take, to attune to others, and to experience empathy. Turning to the terminal only worsens the situation, as the mode of interaction it imposes cripples all those psychological and interpersonal skills necessary to successfully manage this need for social recognition—skills organized by Daniel Goleman as Social Intelligence.[20] Tragically, therefore, as we find ourselves having to perform face-work with faceless others, the terminal mode of interaction prompts, in many, a regressive mode of self-presentation and multiplies the frequency of face-threatening encounters. However, rather than enabling the immediate performance of restorative gestures that could counteract such unfortunate incidents, the terminal mode of interaction offers only mediocre mechanisms to do so. In fact, it is often counterproductive and worsens the situation. This mode of interaction amplifies the impacts of such incidents by enabling their immediate transmissions, by expanding their reach, and by accelerating their velocity. The noxious neural, physical, and psychological impacts of such incidents are not confined to the particular instances when they occur. They gear up the terminal self and set the tone for subsequent interactions, whether at the terminal or face-to-face. However, as Turkle documents, individuals are decreasingly comfortable in, knowledgeable about, and skilled at face-to-face interaction, especially for matters of conflict-resolution.

If Google Earth blurs people's faces and converts them into silhouettes, we should be wary of not too casually replicating this moral optic in our routine terminal interactions with real others. For Levinas, the other's face summons the ethical dimension of human interaction.[21] However, because many terminal interactions conceal users' faces, they inherently dehumanize them; they promote what Zuboff calls a "formal indifference."[22] This type of de-humanization is 'soft,' subtle, and often casually dismissed as a benign or incidental side-effect of our online-life, or as the 'new normal.' However, I believe that it is critically important for the terminal self to recognize this sensibility for what it is, and to refuse the facile, fun, and personalized adjustment to it.

One way of resisting this 'preferred encoding' is to acknowledge how terminal interactions with faceless others change our ethical relations to them, both at the terminal and away from it. Nurturing this awareness should include attention to how we *experience* the faceless other, how we *respond* to him and her, how we *rationalize* our response, and how such routine behaviors help legitimize a new technologically-induced 'common-sense.' On the practical side, nurturing this awareness should also include honest—and face-to-face—conversations with each other about our terminal interactions.[23] Since relying on terminal interactions to resolve face-threatening incidents is notoriously inefficient, weak, and even counterproductive, and since the adverse effects of such incidents carry over in our face-to-face interactions, it only seems logical that we use the latter to resolve the former. 'Face-ing' those we routinely interact with at the terminal will remind us of their full existence. It will enable us to provide them with authentic social recognition, and prompt us to attend to the ethical implications of our human interactions.

Proxie servers

If de-humanization might seem like an incidental outcome of the terminal mode of interaction, it is the purposeful objective of the digital apparatus. For social psychologist Zuboff, the new power unleashed by surveillance capitalism is not a "*coup d'état*" but a "*coup des gens.*"[24] It does not overthrow institutions but people. And by casually delegating human functions, decisions, and responsibilities to the digital apparatus, we accelerate the de-humanization of society and expedite our own disappearance. As Carr notes, this apparatus is quickly repositioning humans in the supporting roles of machines, and in that scenario, humans can't compete. They "are the weak links in the networked system … they can't keep up with computer chatter; they just slow down the conversation."[25] For Ebert, "the human being is actually disappearing from his own society, just as the automobile long ago caused him to disappear from the streets of his cities."[26] Apple's co-founder Steve Wozniak half-humorously wonders "whether he is destined to be a family pet for robot overlords."[27]

The digital apparatus is not only evolving in its abilities to perform mental, affective, and physical functions that were up until now believed to be the hallmark of human intelligence, it is also mutating, and faster than we can understand or control. At some level, the 'automated killing machines' decried by the leaders of the computer industry are the conspicuous and terrifying foot soldiers of a less dramatic digital apparatus that functions with algorithmic 'formal indifference.' However, this formal indifference could also unexpectedly mutate into a very different orientation. As Tesla CEO Elon Musk pointed out at a meeting of the National Governors Association, "Artificial Intelligence is a fundamental existential risk for human civilization" and is the "scariest problem humanity faces."[28]

Undo

> There is no need to fear or hope, but only to look for new weapons.[29]

Because the dangers unleashed by the digital apparatus materialize in various spheres of society, their solutions will similarly have to be specific to the spheres in which they occur. Thus, some of these dangers will require political decisions, others will require legal settlements, economic resolutions, technological applications, educational transformations, etc. Regardless of their forms or spheres, however, developing such solutions necessitates cognition, intelligent communication, and collaboration. As scholars of social movements suggest, effective collective action also necessitates identification, commitment, a shared vision, and other indicators of intrapersonal and interpersonal intelligence. Yet, our near-complete (and personalized) coupling with terminals deteriorates those very intelligences. As symbolic interactionists and others maintain, those can only develop in interaction with co-present and responsive human beings. By deteriorating this essential mechanism of human organization, terminal interactions not only distort users' subjective experiences and social relations, they also weaken their ability to mount a successful resistance against the digital apparatus. Effective resistance must also—and especially—take place at the simple level of interaction. Without it, it is doubtful that the necessary interventions in other societal domains can occur. Accordingly, unless the terminal self cultivates those uniquely human intelligences and reclaims the mode of interaction, s/he will indeed be terminal.

Notes

1 SNCB is the acronym of the Société Nationale des Chemins de fer de Belgique—the Belgian national railroad company.
2 See Dyens (2001).
3 Virilio, Kittler, and Armitage (1999), 87.
4 See especially Bauerlin (2011); Carr (2011, 2015); Jackson (2009); Rheingold (2012); Rushkoff (2011, 2013); and Turkle (2011).
5 Anderson and Rainer (2014).
6 For a comprehensive list of such organizations protecting privacy, see: https://epic.org/privacy/privacy_resources_faq.html#Privacy_Organizations.
7 Fuchs (2017), 342.
8 Fuchs (2017), 346.
9 See especially Turkle (2015).
10 Arluke and Sanders (1996).
11 Irvine (2004).
12 Weigert (1997).
13 Virilio, Kittler, and Armitage (1999).
14 As recent research by Tromhot (2016, 665) reveals, "quitting Facebook leads to higher levels of both cognitive and affective well-being," especially for those who used Facebook passively, extensively, and experiencing envy.
15 Rainie and Anderson (2017), 7.
16 Greenfield (2017).
17 Fuchs (2017), 178.
18 Jauréguiberry (2014).
19 Eggers (2014), 490.
20 Goleman (2006). The eight components of social intelligence consist of: primal empathy, empathic accuracy, attunement, social cognition, synchrony, self-presentation, influence, and concern. The only component that could minimally be present in the terminal mode of interaction is "self-presentation."

21 Honneth (2007).
22 Zuboff (2015), 73.
23 Turkle (2015).
24 Zuboff (2015), 83.
25 Carr (2015), 197.
26 Ebert (2011), 162.
27 Dowd (2017).
28 Domonoske (2017).
29 Deleuze (1992), 4.

References

Anderson, Janna and Lee Rainer. 2014. "Net Threats." Pew Research Internet Project. July 3. www.pewinternet.org/2014/07/03/netthreats/?utm_source=Pew+Internet+Newsletter&utm_campaign=7571aa65d3-Net_Threats_070314&utm_medium=e.

Arluke, Arnold and Clint Sanders. 1996. *Regarding Animals*. Philadelphia, PA: Temple University Press.

Bauerlin, Mark (ed.) 2011. *The Digital Divide: Arguments for and Against Facebook, Google, Texting, and the Age of Social Networking*. New York: Jeremy P. Tarcher.

Carr, Nicholas. 2011. *The Shallows: What the Internet is Doing to Our Brains*. New York: W. W. Norton & Co.

Carr, Nicholas. 2015. *The Glass Cage: Where Automation is Taking Us*. London: The Bodley Head.

Deleuze, Gilles. 1992. "Postscript on the Societies of Control." *October* 59: 3–7.

Domonoske Camila. 2017. "Elon Musk Warns Governors: Artificial Intelligence Poses 'Existential Risk'." www.npr.org/2017/07/17/537686649/elon-musk-warns-governors-artificial-intelligence-poses-existential-risk. Retrieved July 18, 2017.

Dowd, Maureen. 2017. "Elon Musk's Billion-Dollar Crusade to Stop the A.I. Apocalypse." *Vanity Fair*. March 26. www.vanityfair.com/news/2017/03/elon-musk-billion-dollar-crusade-to-stop-ai-space-x. Retrieved July 18, 2017.

Dyens, Ollivier. 2001. *Metal and Flesh: Technology Takes Over*. Cambridge, MA: MIT Press.

Ebert, John David. 2011. *The New Media Invasion: Digital Technologies and the World They Unmake*. Jefferson, NC: McFarlane.

Eggers, Dave. 2014. *The Circle*. New York: Vintage.

Fuchs, Christian. 2017. *Social Media: A Critical Introduction*. Los Angeles: Sage.

Goleman, Daniel. 2006. *Social Intelligence: Beyond IQ, Beyond Emotional Intelligence*. New York: Bantam.

Greenfield, Adam. 2017. *Radical Technologies: The Design of Everyday Life*. Verso. Available at: https://longreads.com/2017/06/13/a-sociology-of-the-smartphone/. Retrieved June 14, 2017.

Honneth, Axel. 2007. *Disrespect: The Normative Foundations of Critical Theory*. Cambridge, UK: Polity.

Irvine, Leslie. 2004. "A Model of Animal Selfhood: Expanding Interactionist Possibilities." *Symbolic Interaction* 27(1): 3–21.

Jackson, Maggie. 2009. *Distracted: The Erosion of Attention and the Coming Dark Age*. New York: Prometheus.

Jauréguiberry, Francis. 2014. "La Déconnection aux Technologies de Communication." *La Découverte-Réseaux* 186(4): 15–49.

Rainie, Lee and Janna Anderson. 2017. "Code-Dependent: Pros and Cons of the Algorithm Age." Pew Research Center, February 2017. Available at: www.pew internet.org/2017/02/08/code-dependent-pros-and-cons-of-the-algorithm-age.

Rheingold, Howard. 2012. *NetSmart: How To Thrive Online*. Cambridge, MA: MIT Press.

Rushkoff, Douglas. 2011. *Program or be Programmed: Ten Commands for a Digital Age*. Berkeley, CA: Soft Skull Press.

Rushkoff, Douglas. 2013. *Present Shock: When Everything Happens Now*. New York: Penguin.

Tromholt, Morten. 2016. "The Facebook Experiment: Quitting Facebook Leads to Higher Levels of Well-Being." *Cyberpsychology, Behavior, and Social Networking* 19(11): 661–666.

Turkle, Sherry. 2011. *Alone Together: Why We Demand More of Technology and Less of Each Other*. New York: Basic Books.

Turkle, Sherry. 2015. *Reclaiming Conversation: The Power of Talk in the Digital Age*. New York: Penguin.

Virilio, Paul, Friedrich Kittler, and John Armitage. 1999. "The Information Bomb: A Conversation." *Angelaki: Journal of the Theoretical Humanities*, 4(2): 81–90. http://dx.doi.org/10.1080/09697259908572036.

Weigert, Andrew J. 1997. *Self, Interaction and Natural Environment: Refocusing our Eyesight*. Albany: SUNY Press.

Zuboff, Shoshana. 2015. "Big Other: Surveillance Capitalism and the Prospects of an Information Civilization." *Journal of Information Technology* (30): 75–89.

Bibliography

Aboujaoude, Elias. 2011. *Virtually You: The Dangerous Powers of the E-Personality*. New York: W. W. Norton & Co.

Acquisiti, Alessandro. 2011. "Les Comportements de Vie Privée Face au Commerce Électronique." *Réseaux* 167: 107–130.

Anderson, Elijah. 2011. *The Cosmopolitan Canopy: Race and Civility in Everyday Life*. New York: W. W. Norton & Co.

Anderson, Janna and Lee Rainer. 2014. "Net Threats." Pew Research Internet Project. July 3. www.pewinternet.org/2014/07/03/netthreats/?utm_source=Pew+ Internet+Newsletter&utm_campaign=7571aa65d3-Net_Threats_070314&utm_ medium=e.

Andrejevic, Mark. 2007. *iSpy: Surveillance and Power in the Interactive Era*. Lawrence, KS: University Press of Kansas.

Andrejevic, Mark. 2013. *Infoglut: How Too Much Information Is Changing the Way We Think and Know*. New York: Routledge.

Aries, Phillipe. 1965. *Centuries of Childhood: A Social History of Family Life*. New York: Vintage.

Arluke, Arnold and Clint Sanders. 1996. *Regarding Animals*. Philadelphia, PA: Temple University Press.

Ascher, François. 2000. *La Société Hypermoderne*. Paris: Éditions de l'Aube.

Ascher, François. 2007. *Examen Clinique: Journal d'Un Hypermoderne*. Paris: Éditions de l'Aube.

Ascher, François. 2012. "La Société Hypermoderne." *Société Digitale*. www.culture mobile.net/quotidien-intelligent/individu-hypermoderne.

Asimov, Isaac. 2008. *I, Robot*. New York: Spectra.

Aubert, Nicole and Claudine Haroche. 2011 "Être Visible pour Exister: L'Injonction à la Visibilité." pp. 7–22 in *Les Tyrannies de la Visibilité: Être Visible Pour Exister?*, Nicole Aubert and Claudine Haroche (eds.). Toulouse: Érès.

Aubert, Nicole. 2003. *Le Culte de l'Urgence: La Société Malade du Temps*. Paris: Flammarion.

Aubert, Nicole. 2005a. "Un Individu Paradoxal." pp. 13–24 in *L'Individu Hypermoderne*, Nicole Aubert (ed.). Toulouse: Érès.

Aubert, Nicole. 2005b. "L'Intensité de Soi." pp. 73–87 in *L'Individu Hypermoderne*, Nicole Aubert (ed.). Toulouse: Érès.

Aubert, Nicole. 2006a. "Sur L'hypermodernité et de la Société Hypermoderne." *Next Modernity* 10: 30.

Aubert, Nicole. 2006b. "Hyperformance et Combustion de Soi." *Études* 405(10): 339–351.

Aubert, Nicole. 2008a. "Violence du Temps et Pathologies Hypermodernes." *Cliniques Méditerranéennes* 78: 23–38.

Aubert, Nicole. 2008b. "Les Pathologies Hypermodernes: Expressions d'Une Nouvelle Normalité?" *Revue Internationale de Sociologie* 18(3): 419–426.

Balbus, Isaac D. 2005. *Mourning and Identity: Essays in the Psychoanalysis of Contemporary Society*. New York: Otherness.

Ball, Kirstie. 2009. "Exposure: Exploring the Subject of Surveillance." *Information, Communication and Society* 12(5): 639–657.

Barber, Benjamin. 2008. *Consumed: How Markets Corrupt Children, Infantilize Adults, and Swallow Citizens Whole*. New York: W. W. Norton & Co.

Bardhi, Fleura and Giana M. Eckhardt. 2012. "Access-Based Consumption: The Case of Car Sharing." *Journal of Consumer Research* 39(4): 881–898.

Barker, Collin 2014. "25 Billion Devices by 2020 to Build the Internet of Things." ZDNet November 1. Accessible at: www.zdnet.com/article/25-billion-connected-devices-by-2020-to-build-the-internet-of-things. Retrieved November 13, 2014.

Baruch, Yehuda. 2005. "Bullying on the Net: Adverse Behavior on E-mail and its Impact." *Information and Management* 42: 361–371.

Barus-Michel, Jacqueline. 2005. "L'Hypermodernité, Dépassement ou Perversion de la Modernité?" pp. 246–247 in *L'Individu Hypermoderne*, Nicole Aubert (ed.). Toulouse: Érès.

Barus-Michel, Jacqueline. 2005. "L'Hypermodernité, Dépassement ou Perversion de la Modernité?" pp. 246–247 in *L'Individu Hypermoderne*, Nicole Aubert (ed.). Toulouse: Érès.

Baudrillard, Jean. 2010. *The Agony of Power*. Cambridge, MA: MIT Press (Semiotext(e)).

Bauerlin, Mark (ed.) 2011. *The Digital Divide: Arguments for and Against Facebook, Google, Texting, and the Age of Social Networking*. New York: Jeremy P. Tarcher.

Bauman, Zygmunt and David Lyon. 2013. *Liquid Surveillance*. Cambridge, UK: Polity.

Bauman, Zygmunt and Leonidas Donskis. 2013. *Moral Blindness: The Loss of Sensibility in Liquid Modernity*. Cambridge, UK: Polity.

Bauman, Zygmunt. 2000. *Liquid Modernity*. Cambridge, UK: Polity.

Bauman, Zygmunt. 2005. *Liquid Life*. Cambridge, UK: Polity.

Bauman, Zygmunt. 2007. *Consuming Life*. Cambridge, UK: Polity.

Baym, Nancy K. 2010. *Personal Connection in the Digital Age*. Cambridge, UK: Polity.

Baym, Nancy K. and danah boyd. 2012. "Socially Mediated Publicness: An Introduction." *Journal of Broadcasting & Electronic Media* 56(3): 320–329.

Beer, David. 2009. "Power through the Algorithm? Participatory Web Cultures and the *Technological Unconscious*." *New Media & Society* 11(6): 985–1002.

Belk, Russel. 2000. "May the Farce be With You: On Las Vegas and Consumer Infantilization." *Consumption, Markets and Culture* 4(2): 101–124.

Bennett, Colin. 2015. "Trends in Voter Surveillance in Western Societies: Privacy Intrusion and Democratic Implications." *Surveillance & Society* 13(3): 370–384.

Berman, Morris. 2000. *The Twilight of American Culture*. New York: W. W. Norton & Co.

Berman, Morris. 2006. *Dark Ages America: The Final Phase of Empire*. New York: W. W. Norton & Co.

Bernardini, Jacopo. 2014. "The Infantilization of the Postmodern Adult and the Figure of Kidult." *Postmodern Openings* 5(2): 39–55.

Blanchard, Anita. 2004. "Virtual Behavior Settings: An Application of Behavior Setting Theories to Virtual Communities." *Journal of Computer-Mediated Communication* 9(2).

Blatterer, Harry. 2007. "Contemporary Adulthood: Reconceptualizing an Uncontested Category." *Current Sociology*, 55: 771–792.

Bodford, Jessica E., Virginia S. Y. Kwan, and David S. Sobota. 2017. "Fatal Attractions: Attachment to Smartphones Predicts Anthropomorphic Beliefs and Dangerous Behaviors." *Cyberpsychology, Behavior, and Social Networking*, 20(5): 320–326.

Boghosian, John Arden. 2003. *America's Meltdown: The Lower-Common-Denominator Society*. Westport, CT: Praeger.

Bugeja, Michael. 2005. *Interpersonal Divide: The Search for Community in a Technological Age*. New York: Oxford University Press.

Calcutt, Andrew. 2000. *Arrested Development: Pop Culture and the Erosion of Adulthood*. London and New York: Cassell.

Carr, Nicholas. 2011. *The Shallows: What the Internet is Doing to Our Brains*. New York: W. W. Norton & Co.

Carr, Nicholas. 2015. *The Glass Cage: Where Automation is Taking Us*. London: The Bodley Head.

Castel, Robert. 2005. "La Face Cachée de l'individu Hypermoderne: L'individu par Défaut." pp. 119–128 in N. Aubert (ed.). *L'Individu Hypermoderne*. Toulouse: Erès.

Castells, Manuel. 2006. "The Network Society: From Knowledge to Policy." pp. 3–21 in *The Network Society: From Knowledge to Policy*, Manuel Castell and Gustavo Cardoso (eds.). Washington, D.C.: Center for Transnational Relations.

Charles, Sébastien. 2009. "For a Humanism Amid Hypermodernity: From a Society of Knowledge to a Critical Knowledge of Society." *Axiomathes* 19: 389–400.

Collet, Peter and Peter Marsh. 1981. "Patterns of Public Behavior: Collision Avoidance on a Pedestrian Crossing." pp. 199–218 in *Nonverbal Communication, Interaction, and Gesture*, Adam Kendon et al. (eds.). The Hague: Mouton.

Cooper, Anderson. 2017. "What is Brain Hacking? Tech Insiders on Why You Should Care." *60 Minutes*. CBS. June 11. www.cbsnews.com/news/what-is-brain-hacking-tech-insiders-on-why-you-should-care/.

Côté, James. 2000. *Arrested Adulthood: The Changing Nature of Maturity and Identity*. New York: New York University Press.

Cournut, Jean. 2005. "Les Défoncés." pp. 61–71 in *L'Individu Hypermoderne*, Nicole Aubert (ed.). Toulouse: Érès.

Cross, Gary. 2008. *Men to Boys: The Making of Modern Immaturity*. New York: Columbia University Press.

Cupach, William R. and Sandra Metts. 1994. *Face-work*. Thousand Oaks, CA: Sage.

Czerwinski, Mary, Eric Horvitz, and Susan Wilhite. 2004. "A Diary Study of Task Switching and Interruptions." Proceedings of the SIGCHI Conference on Human Factors in Computing Systems. New York: ACM.

Daly, Steven and Nathaniel Wice. 1995. *alt.culture: An A-to-Z Guide to the 90s—Underground, Online, and Over-the-Counter*. New York: Harper-Perennial.

Darley, John. M. and Bibb Latané. 1968. "Bystander Intervention in Emergencies: Diffusion of Responsibility." *Journal of Personality and Social Psychology* 8: 377–383.

Dator, James A., John A. Sweeney, and Aubrey M. Yee. 2015. *Mutative Media: Communication Technologies and Power Relations in the Past, Present, and Futures*. Lecture Notes in Social Networks. Switzerland: Springer International Publishing.

De Gaulejac, Vincent. 2005. "Le Sujet Manqué: L'Individu face aux Contradictions de l'Hypermodernité." pp. 129–143 in *L'Individu Hypermoderne*, Nicole Aubert (ed.). Toulouse: Érès.

De Gaulejac, Vincent. 2011. "Entre Dissimulation et ostentation: Le Traitement de l'Envie dans les Sociétés contemporaines." pp. 245–257 in *Les Tyrannies de la Visibilité: Être Visible Pour Exister?*, Nicole Aubert and Claudine Haroche (eds.). Toulouse: Erès.

Deleuze, Gilles. 1992. "Postscript on the Societies of Control." *October* 59: 3–7.

Derks, Daantje and Arnold B. Bakker. 2010. "The Impact of E-Mail Communication on Organizational Life." *Cyberpsychology: Journal of Psychosocial Research on Cyberspace* 4(1). Retrieved December 12, 2013. file://localhost/(http://cyberpsychology.eu:view.php%3Fcisloclanku=2010052401&article=1).

Dery, Mark. 1999. *The Pyrotechnic Insanitarium: American Culture on the Brink*. New York: Grove Press.

Domenici, Kathy and Stephen W. Littlejohn. 2006. *Face-work: Bridging Theory and Practice*. Thousand Oaks, CA: Sage.

Domonoske Camila. 2016. "Students Have 'Dismaying' Inability To Tell Fake News From Real, Study Finds." KNPR. Retrieved November 23, 2016. www.npr.org/sections/thetwo-way/2016/11/23/503129818/study-finds-students-have-dismaying-inability-to-tell-fake-news-from-real.

Domonoske Camila. 2017. "Elon Musk Warns Governors: Artificial Intelligence Poses 'Existential Risk'." www.npr.org/2017/07/17/537686649/elon-musk-warns-governors-artificial-intelligence-poses-existential-risk. Retrieved July 18, 2017.

Donnath, Judith. 2017. "The Robot Dog Fetches for Whom?" https://medium.com/berkman- klein-center/the-robot-dog-fetches-for-whom-a9c1dd0a458a. Retrieved June 15, 2017.

Dowd, Maureen. 2017. "Elon Musk's Billion-Dollar Crusade to Stop the A.I. Apocalypse." *Vanity Fair*. March 26. www.vanityfair.com/news/2017/03/elon-musk-billion-dollar-crusade-to-stop-ai-space-x. Retrieved July 18, 2017.

Dubey, Gérard. 2001. "Les Systèmes d'Information et de Communication ou Comment les Sociétés Se Pensent." pp. 273–285 in N*ouvelles Technologies et Modes de Vie: Aliénation ou Hypermodernité?*, Philippe Moati (ed.). Paris: Éditions de l'Aube.

Dubey, Gérard. 2001. *Le Lien Social à l'ère du Virtuel*. Paris: Presses Universitaires de France.

Dufour, Robert-Danny. 2008. *The Art of Shrinking Heads: On the New Servitude of the Liberated in the Age of Total Capitalism*. Cambridge, UK: Polity Press.

Dyens, Ollivier. 2001. *Metal and Flesh: Technology Takes Over*. Cambridge, MA: MIT Press.

Ebert, John David. 2011. *The New Media Invasion: Digital Technologies and the World They Unmake*. Jefferson, NC: McFarlane.

Eggers, David. 2014. *The Circle*. New York: Vintage.

Ehrenberg, Alain. 2000. *La Fatigue D'Être Soi*. Paris: Odile Jacob.

Ellul, Jacques. 1964. *The Technological Society*. New York: Alfred A. Knopf.

Eriksen, Thomas Hylland. 2001. *The Tranny of the Moment: Fast and Slow Time in the Information Age*. London: Pluto Press.

Fox, Jesse and Margaret C. Rooney. 2015. "The Dark Triad and Trait Self-objectifications as Predictors of Men's Use and Self-Presentation Behaviors on Social Networking Sites." *Personality and Individual Differences* 76: 161–165.

Franks, David. 2003. "Mutual Interests, Different Lenses: Current Neuroscience and Symbolic Interaction." *Symbolic Interaction* 26(4): 613–630.

Friedman, Raymond and Steven C. Currall. 2003. "Conflict Escalation: Dispute Exacerbating Elements of E-mail Communication." *Human Relations* 56(11): 1325–1347.

Fuchs, Christian. 2017. *Social Media: A Critical Introduction*. Los Angeles: Sage.

Furedi, Frank. 2004. Therapy *Culture: Cultivating Vulnerability in an Uncertain Age.* London: Routledge.

Gabriele Alex. 2008. "A Sense of Belonging and Exclusion: 'Touchability' and 'Untouchability' in Tamil Nadu." *Ethnos*, 73(4): 523–543.

Gane, Nicholas. 2006. "Speed Up or Slow Down? Social Theory in the Information Age." *Information, Communication & Society* 9(1): 20–38.

Gane, Nicholas. 2011. "How the Internet Gets Inside Us." *The New Yorker*. Retrieved February 14, 2014. www.newyorker.com/magazine/2011/02/14/the-information.

Gardner, Howard and Katie Davis. 2013. *The App Generation: How Today's Youth Navigate Identity, Intimacy, and Imagination in a Digital World*. New Haven, CT: Yale University Press.

Gardner, Howard. 2006. *Changing Minds*. Boston: Harvard Business School Press.

Gauchet, Marcel. "Vers une Mutation Anthropologique?" pp. 290–301 in *L'Individu Hypermoderne*, Nicole Aubert (ed.). Toulouse: Érès.

Gillath, Omri. In press. *Adult Attachment: A Concise Introduction to Theory and Research*. Washington: Academic Press.

Gillespie, Tarleton. 2003. "The Stories Digital Tools Tell." pp. 1–21 in *New Media: Theses on Convergence Media and Digital Reproduction*, John Caldwell and Anna Everett (eds.). New York and London: Routledge.

Giraldi, William. 2015. "Object Lesson: Why We Need Physical Books." *New Republic*, Retrieved April 19. www.newrepublic.com/article/121560/bibliophiles-defense-physical-books.

Gitlin, Todd. 2011. "Nomadicity." pp. 207–214, in *The Digital Divide: Arguments for and Against Facebook, Google, Texting, and the Age of Social Networking*, Mark Bauerlein (ed.). New York: Jeremy P. Tarcher.

Giumetti, Gary W., Eric S. McKibben, Andrea L Hatfield, Amber N. Schroeder, and Robin M. Kowalski. 2012. "Cyberincivility @ Work: The New Age of Interpersonal Deviance." *Cyberpsychology, Behavior and Social Networking* 15(3): 148–154.

Goel, Vindu. 2014. "Facebook Tinkers with Users' Emotions in News Feed Experiment, Stirring Outcry." *New York Times*, Retrieved June 29. www.nytimes.com/2014/06/30/technology/facebook-tinkers-with-users-emotions-in-news-feed-experiment-stirring-outcry.html?_r=0.

Goffman, Erving. 1955. "On Face-Work: An Analysis of Ritual Elements in Social Interaction." *Psychiatry* 18(3): 213–231.

Goleman, Daniel. 2006. *Social Intelligence: Beyond IQ, Beyond Emotional Intelligence*. New York: Bantam.

Gonzales, Amy L. and Jeffrey T. Hancock. 2011. "Mirror, Mirror on my Facebook Wall: Effects of Exposure to Facebook on Self-Esteem." *Cyberpsychology, Behavior, and Social Networking* 14(1–2): 79–83.

Gopnik, Adam. 2011. "How the Internet Gets Inside Us." *The New Yorker*. Retrieved February 14, 2014. www.newyorker.com/magazine/2011/02/14/the-information.

Gopnik, Adam. 2015. "The Outside Game: How the Sociologist Howard Becker Studies the Conventions of the Unconventional." *The New Yorker*. January 12. www.newyorker.com/magazine/2015/01/12/outside-game. Retrieved January 13, 2015.

Gottschalk, Simon and Jennifer Whitmer. 2013. "Hypermodern Dramaturgy in Online Encounters." pp. 309–334 in *The Drama of Social Life: A Dramaturgical Handbook*, Charles Edgley (ed.). Ashgate.

Gottschalk, Simon. 1999. "Speed Culture: Fast Strategies in TV Commercials." *Qualitative Sociology* 22 (4): 311–329.

Gottschalk, Simon. 2009. "Hypermodern Consumption and Megalomania: Superlatives in Commercials." *Journal of Consumer Culture* 9(3): 307–327.

Gottschalk. Simon. 2015. *Interfacework: l'interazione simbolica nell'epoca digitale* [Inter-Face-Work: Symbolic Interaction in the Digital Age]. With an introduction by Giuseppina Cerosimo. Calimera: Edizioni Kurumuny.

Greene, Daniel. 2015. "Drone Vision." *Surveillance & Society* 13(2): 233–249.

Greenfield, Adam. 2017. *Radical Technologies: The Design of Everyday Life*. Verso. Available at: https://longreads.com/2017/06/13/a-sociology-of-the-smartphone/. Retrieved June 14, 2017.

Gustavsson, Bengt. 2005. "The Ethics of Managing Corporate Identity." *Journal of Human Values* 11: 9–29.

Guzman, Javier. 2015. "8 de cada 10 Personas son Incapaces de Hacer Discursos de Un Minuto." *El Pais* July 10. http://elpais.com/elpais/2015/07/30/videos/1438279001_736056.htm.

Hampton, K. N., L. Rainie, W. Lu, M. Dwyer, I. Shin, and K. Purcell. 2014. "Social Media and the Spiral of Silence." Washington D.C.: Pew Research Center.

Haroche, Claudine. 2011. "L'invisibilité Interdite." pp. 77–102 in *Les Tyrannies de la Visibilité: Être Visible Pour Exister?*, Nicole Aubert and Claudine Haroche (eds.). Toulouse: Érès.

Harris, Michael. 2014. *The End of Absence: Reclaiming What We've Lost in a World of Constant Connection*. New York: Current.

Hassan, Robert. 2009. *Empires of Speed: Time and the Acceleration of Politics in Society*. Leiden: Brill.

Hassan, Robert. 2012. *The Age of Distraction*. New Brunswick: Transactions.

Hastings, Sally O. 2009. "Embarrassing E-mails in Organizations: Exploring Online Embarrassment and Identity Management." *Journal of Creative Communications* 4(1): 33–43.

Hayles, N. Katherine. 2012. *How We Think: Digital Media and Contemporary Technogenesis*. University of Chicago Press.

Hebdige, Dick. 2003. "Dis-Gnosis: Disney and the Re-Tooling of Knowledge, Art, Culture, Life, Etc." *Cultural Studies* 17(2): 150–167.

Heritage, John and David Greatbatch. 1986. "Generating Applause: A Study of Rhetoric and Response at Party Political Conferences." *American Journal of Sociology* 92(1): 110–157.

Hochschild, Arlie R. 2016. *Strangers in Their Own Land: Anger and Mourning on the American Right*. New York: New Press.

Honneth, Axel. 1992. "Integrity and Disrespect: Principles of a Conception of Morality Based on the Theory of Recognition." *Political Theory* 29(2): 187–201.

Honneth, Axel. 1995. *The Struggle for Recognition: The Moral Grammar of Social Conflicts*. Cambridge, UK: Polity Press.

Honneth, Axel. 2007. *Disrespect: The Normative Foundations of Critical Theory.* Cambridge, UK: Polity.

Irvine, Leslie. 2004. "A Model of Animal Selfhood: Expanding Interactionist Possibilities." *Symbolic Interaction* 27(1): 3–21.

Jackson, Maggie. 2009. *Distracted: The Erosion of Attention and the Coming Dark Age.* New York: Prometheus.

Jappe, Anselm. 1999. "Sic Transit Gloria Artis: 'The End of Art' for Theodor Adorno and Guy Debord." *Substance* 90: 102–128.

Jauréguiberry, Francis. 2003a. *Les Branchés du Portable.* Paris: Presse Universitaire Française.

Jauréguiberry, Francis. 2003b "Internet Comme Espace Inédit de Construction de Soi." pp. 223–244 in *L'Internet, Nouvel Espace Citoyen?*, Francis Jauréguiberry and Serge Proulx (eds.). Paris: l'Harmattan.

Jauréguiberry, Francis. 2004. "Hypermobilité et Télécommunication." pp. 130–138 in *Les Sens du Mouvement: Modernité et Mobilités dans les Sociétés Urbaines Contemporaines*, S. Allemand, F. Ascher, and J. Lévy (eds.). Paris: Belin.

Jauréguiberry, Francis. 2005. "L'Immédiaté Télécommunicationnelle." pp. 85–98 in *Nouvelles Technologies et Modes de Vie: Aliénation ou Hypermodernité?*, Philippe Moati (ed.). Paris: Éditions de l'Aube.

Jauréguiberry, Francis. 2014. "La Déconnection aux Technologies de Communication." *La Découverte-Réseaux* 186(4): 15–49.

Joinson, Adam, N. 2007. "Disinhibition and the Internet." pp. 43–60 in *Psychology and the Internet: Intrapersonal, Interpersonal, and Transpersonal Implications*, J. Gayckenback (ed.). Burlington, MA: Elsevier.

Kalman, Yoram and Sheizaf Rafaeli. 2011. "Online Pauses and Silence: Chronemic Expectancy Violations in Written Computer-Mediated Communication." *Communication Research* 38(1): 54–69.

Kanungo, Shiraj and Vikas Jain. 2008. "Modeling Email Use: A Case of Email System Transition." *Systems Dynamics Review* 24(3): 299–319.

Keen, Andrew. 2012. *Digital Vertigo: How Today's Online Social Revolution is Dividing, Diminishing, and Disorienting Us.* New York: St. Martin Griffin.

Khullar, Dhruv. 2016. "How Social Isolation Is Killing Us." *New York Times.* www.nytimes.com/2016/12/22/upshot/how-social-isolation-is-killing-us.html.

King, Storm A. and Danielle Moreggi. 2007. "Internet Self-Help and Support Groups: The Pros and Cons of Text-Based Mutual Aid." pp. 221–244 in *Psychology and the Internet: Intrapersonal, Interpersonal, and Transpersonal Implications*, J. Gayckenback (ed.). Burlington, MA: Elsevier.

Kramer, Adam, D., Jamie E. Guillory, and Jeffrey T. Hancock. 2014. "Experimental Evidence of Massive-Scale Emotional Contagion through Social Networks." *Proceedings of the National Academy of Sciences* 111(24): 8788–8790.

Kruger, Justin, Nicholas Epley, Jason Parker, and Zhi-Wen Ng. 2005. "Egocentrism over E-mail: Can we Communicate as well as we Think?" *Journal of Personality and Social Psychology* 89(6): 925–936.

Kurtzberg, Terri R., Charles E. Naquin, and Liuba Y. Belkin. 2005. "Electronic Performance Appraisals: The Effects of E-mail Communication on Peer Ratings in Actual and Simulated Environments." *Organizational Behavior and Human Decision Processes* 98(2): 216–226.

Kurzweil, Ray. (ed.). 1990. *The Age of Intelligent Machines.* Cambridge, MA: MIT Press.

Lanier, Jaron. 2010. *You are Not a Gadget: A Manifesto.* New York: Vintage.

Levi-Strauss, Claude. 1946. "La Technique du Bonheur aux USA." *Age D'Or* 1: 75–83.

Levy, Matthew. 2011. "A Notion of Faces, Not Laws: Facebook as Ideological Platform." *Fast Capitalism* 8(1): Retrieved June 11, 2015. www.uta.edu/huma/agger/fastcapitalism/8_1/levy8_1.html.

Lim, Vivien K. G. and Teo Thompson. 2009. "Mind Your E-Manners: Impact of Cyber-Incivility on Employees' Work Attitudes and Behaviors." *Information and Management* 46: 419–425.

Ling, Rich. 2010. "Texting as a Life Phase Medium." *Journal of Computer-Mediated Communication* 15: 277–292.

Lipovetsky, Gilles. 1983. *L' Ère du Vide: Essais sur L'individualisme Contemporain.* Paris: Gallimard.

Lipovetsky, Gilles. 2006. *Le Bonheur Paradoxal: Essai sur la Société d'Hyperconsommation.* Paris: Gallimard.

Lynch, Michael Patrick. 2016. *The Internet of Us: Knowing More and Understanding Less in the Age of Big Data.* New York: Liveright.

Manning, Phillip. 2005. *Freud and American Sociology.* Cambridge, UK: Polity.

Manovich, Lev. 2013. "The Algorithms of Our Lives." *Chronicle of Higher Education.* Retrieved December 19, 2013 http://chronicle.com/article/The-Algorithms-of-Our-Lives-/143557/?cid=at&utm_source=at&utm_medium=en.

Mariani, Mike. 2016. "The Antisocial Network." *Psychology Today* 49(5): 80–88.

Martynnova, Irina A. and Gennady V. Glukhov. 2015. "Exploring the Echoes of Social Changes: Case Study of Language Infantilism." *Mediterranean Journal of Social Sciences* 6(6): 315–322.

Marwick, Alice and danah boyd. 2010. "I Tweet Honestly, I Tweet Passionately: Twitter Users, Context Collapse, and the Imagined Audience." *New Media & Society* 13(1): 114–133.

Marx, Gary T. 2007. "Soft Surveillance: The Growth of Mandatory Volunteerism in Collecting Personal Information." pp. 37–56 in *Surveillance and Security: Technological Politics and Power in Everyday Life*, T. Monahan (ed.). London: Routledge.

Marx, Gary T. 2016. *Windows into the Soul: Surveillance and Society in an Age of High Technology.* University of Chicago Press.

Maslow, Abraham. 1962. *Toward a Psychology of Being.* New York: Van Nostrand.

Mayer-Schonberger, Viktor. 2011. *Delete: The Virtue of Forgetting in the Digital Age.* Princeton, NJ: Princeton University Press.

Naquin, Charles E., Terri R. Kurtzberg, and Liuba Y. Belkin. 2008. "E-mail Communication and Group Cooperation in Mixed Motive Contexts." *Social Justice Research* 21(4): 470–489.

Naquin, Charles E., Terri R. Kurtzberg, and Liuba Y. Belkin. 2010. "The Finer Points of Lying Online: E-mail versus Pen and Paper." *Journal of Applied Psychology* 95(2): 387–394.

New York Times Editorial Board. 2016. "Facebook and the Digital Virus Called Fake News" November 19. Retrieved November 20, 2016. www.nytimes.com/2016/11/20/opinion/sunday/facebook-and-the-digital-virus-called-fake-news.html?hpw&rref=sunday-review&action=click&pgtype=Homepage&module=well-region&region=bottom-well&WT.nav=bottom-well.

Nygren, Katarina Giritli and Katarina L. Gidlund. 2016. "The Pastoral Power of Technology: Rethinking Alienation in Digital Culture." pp. 398–412 in *Marx in the Age of Digital Capitalism*, Christian Fuchs and Vincent Mosco (eds.). Leiden: Brill.

O'Reilly, Jane, Sandra L. Robinson, Jennifer L. Berdahl, and Sara Banki. 2015. "Is Negative Attention Better Than No Attention? The Comparative Effects of Ostracism and Harassment at Work." *Organization Science* 26(3), 774–793.

O'Sullivan, Patrick B. and Andrew J. Flannagin. 2003. "Reconceptualizing 'Flaming' and Other Problematic Messages." *New Media and Society* 5: 69–94.

Obama, Barack H. 2017. Farewell address. January 10.

Olmstead Kenneth and Aaron Smith. 2017. "What the Public Knows About Cybersecurity." Pew Research Center on Internet and American Life March 22. Retrieved June 9, 2017. www.pewinternet.org/2017/03/22/what-the-public-knows-about-cybersecurity/.

Omtzigt, Pieter. 2015. "Mass Surveillance." Parliamentary Assembly, Council of Europe, January 26, 2015. Quoted in Rosamunde Van Brakel, Liliana A. Moliner, and Gemma G. Clavell. "Surveillance: Ambiguities and Asymmetries." *Surveillance & Society* 13(3/4): 324–325.

Pagès, Max. 2005. "Massification, Regression, Violence Dans La Société Contemporaine." pp. 229–238 in *L'Individu Hypermoderne*, Nicole Aubert (ed.). Toulouse: Erès.

Pariser, Eli. 2012. *The Filter Bubble: How the New Personalized Web Is Changing What We Read and How We Think*. New York: Penguin.

Parisi, David. 2008. "'Fingerbombing,' or 'Touching is Good': The Cultural Construction of Technologized Touch." *Senses & Society* 3(3): 307–327.

Pew Research Center. "Online Harassment." Retrieved May 21, 2017. www.pewinternet.org/2014/10/22/online-harassment/ Purcell, Kristen. 2011.

Pew Research Center. 2011. "Search and E-mail Still Top the List of Most Popular Online Activities." Retrieved December 23, 2013. www.pewinternet.org/Reports/2011/Search-and-e-mail.aspx.

Pew Research Center. 2014. "Technology Impact on Workers." Retrieved on February 20, 2017. www.pewInternet.org/2014/12/30/technologys-impact-on-workers/.

Privitera, Carmel and Mary Ann Campbell. 2009. "Cyberbullying: The New Face of Workplace Bullying." *CyberPsychology & Behavior* 12(4): 395–400.

Purcell, Kristen and Lee Rainie. 2014. "Technology's Impact on Workers." Pew Research Center. Retrieved on February 20, 2017. www.pewinternet.org/2014/12/30/technologys-impact-on-workers/.

Purcell, Kristen. 2011. "Search and E-mail Still Top the List of Most Popular Online Activities." Pew Research Center. 2011. Retrieved December 23, 2013. www.pewinternet.org/Reports/2011/Search-and-e-mail.aspx.

Ragnedda, Massimo. 2011. "Social Control and Surveillance in the Society of Consumers." *International Journal of Sociology and Anthropology* 3(6): 180–188.

Rainie, Lee and Barry Wellman. 2012. *Networked: The New Social Operating System*. Cambridge, MA: MIT Press.

Rainie, Lee and Janna Anderson. 2017. "Code-Dependent: Pros and Cons of the Algorithm Age." Pew Research Center, February 2017. Available at: www.pewinternet.org/2017/02/08/code-dependent-pros-and-cons-of-the-algorithm-age.

Rainie, Lee, Janna Anderson, and Jonathan Albright. 2017. "The Future of Free Speech, Trolls, Anonymity, and Fake News Online." Pew Research Center, March 2017. Available at: www.pewinternet.org/2017/03/29/the-future-of-free-speech-trolls-anonymity-and-fake-news-online/. Downloaded June 9, 2017.

Redhead, Steve. 2011. *We Have Never Been Postmodern: Theory at the Speed of Light*. Edinburgh University Press.

Rheingold, Howard. 1992. *Virtual Reality*. New York: Touchstone.

Rheingold, Howard. 2012. *NetSmart: How To Thrive Online*. Cambridge, MA: MIT Press.

Richardson, Ingrid and Amanda Third. 2009. "Cultural Phenomenology and the Material Culture of Mobile Media." pp. 145–156 in *Material Culture and Technology in Every Day: Ethnographic Approaches*, Phillip Vannini (ed.). New York: Peter Lang.

Riva, Giuseppe and Carlo Galimberti (eds.). 2001. *Towards CyberPsychology: Mind, Cognition and Society in the Internet Age*. Amsterdam: IOS.

Roberts, Paul. 2014. *The Impulse Society: America in the Age of Instant Gratification*. New York: Bloomsberry.

Rojek, Chris, 2004. "The Consumerist Syndrome in Contemporary Society: An Interview with Zygmunt Bauman" *Journal of Consumer Culture* 4(3): 291–312.

Rosa, Hartmut. 2010. *Accélération: Une Critique Sociale du Temps*. Paris: La Découverte.

Rosa, Hartmut. 2012. *Aliénation et Accélération: Vers une Théorie Critique de la Modernité Tardive*. Paris: La Découverte.

Rosa, Hartmut. 2013. *Alienation and Acceleration: Towards a Critical Theory of Later Temporality*. Malmögade, Denmark: NSU Press.

Rosa, Hartmut and W. E. Sheuerman (eds.) 2009. *High-Speed Society: Social Acceleration, Power, and Modernity*. Philadelphia, PA: Pennsylvania University Press.

Rosen, Christine. 2007. "Virtual Friendship and the New Narcissism." *The New Atlantis*. Summer.

Rugoff, Ralph. 1995. *Circus Americanus*. London: Verso.

Rushkoff, Douglas. 2011. *Program or be Programmed: Ten Commands for a Digital Age*. Berkeley, CA: Soft Skull Press.

Rushkoff, Douglas. 2013. *Present Shock: When Everything Happens Now*. New York: Penguin.

Scheff, Thomas J. 2000. *Emotions, Nationalism, and War*. Lincoln, NE: iUniverse.

Schwalbe, Michael L. 1989. "Meadian Ethics for Marxist Psychology." *Berkeley Journal of Sociology* 34: 87–104.

Seremetakis, Nadia C. 1994. "The Memory of the Senses, Part I: Marks of the Transitory." pp. 1–18 in *The Senses Still: Perception and Memory as Material Culture in Modernity*, Nadia C. Seremetakis (ed.). Boulder: Westview.

Shalin, Dmitri. 1988. "G. H. Mead, Socialism, and the Progressive Agenda." *American Journal of Sociology* 92: 913–951.

Shipley, David and Will Schwalbe. 2008. *Send: Why People E-mail So Badly and How To Do It Better*. New York: Vantage.

Simmel, Georg. 1965. "The Metropolis and Mental Life." pp. 409–424 in *The Sociology of Georg Simmel*, K. H. Wolff (ed.). New York: Free Press.

Spurk, Jan. 2011. "De La Reconaissance á l'Insignificance." pp. 323–333 in *Les Tyrannies de la Visibilité: Être Visible Pour Exister?*, Nicole Aubert and Claudine Haroche (eds.). Toulouse: Érès.

Stephens, Keri K., Marian L. Houser, and Renee L. Cowan. 2009. "R U Able to MeatMe?: The Impact of Students' Overly Casual E-mail Messages to Instructors." *Communication Education* 58(3): 303–326.

Streitfeld, David. 2017. "'The Internet Is Broken': @ev Is Trying to Salvage It." *New York Times*. May 21, 2017. www.nytimes.com/2017/05/20/technology/evan-williams-medium-twitter-internet.html.

Tapia, Claude. 2012. "Modernité, Postmodernité, Hypermodernité." *Connexions* 1: 15–25.

Tisseron, Serge. 2008. *Virtuel, Mon Amour: Penser, Aimer, Souffrir à l'Ère des Nouvelles Technologies*. Paris: Albin Michel.

Tisseron, Serge. 2011a. "Les Nouveaux Réseaux Sociaux: Visibilité et Invisibilité sur le Net." pp. 119–130 in *Les Tyrannies de la Visibilité: Être Visible Pour Exister?* Nicole Aubert and Claudine Haroche (eds.). Toulouse: Erès.

Tisseron, Serge. 2011b. "Intimité et Extimité." *Communications* 1(88): 83–91.

Tromholt, Morten. 2016. "The Facebook Experiment: Quitting Facebook Leads to Higher Levels of Well-Being." *Cyberpsychology, Behavior, and Social Networking* 19(11): 661–666.

Turkle, Sherry. 2009. *Simulation and Its Discontents*. Cambridge, MA: MIT Press.

Turkle, Sherry. 2011. *Alone Together: Why We Demand More of Technology and Less of Each Other*. New York: Basic Books.

Turkle, Sherry. 2015. *Reclaiming Conversation: The Power of Talk in the Digital Age*. New York: Penguin.

Turnage, Anna K. 2008. "Email Flaming Behavior and Organizational Conflict." *Journal of Computer Mediated Communication* 13: 43–59.

U.S. Civil Rights Congress. 1970. *We Charge Genocide: The Historic Petition to the United Nations for Relief from a Crime of the United States Government against the Negro people*. New York: International Publishers.

Van Brakel, Rosamunde, Liliana A. Moliner, and Gemma G. Clavell. 2015. "Surveillance: Ambiguities and Asymmetries." *Surveillance & Society* 13(3/4): 324–326.

Van den Bergh, Bert. 2013. "Depression: Resisting Ultra-Liberalism?" pp. 81–102 in *The Social Pathologies of Contemporary Civilization*, Kieran Keohane and Anders Petersen (eds.). Farnham, UK: Ashgate.

Van Koningsbruggen, Guido M., Tilo Hartmann, Allison Eden, and Harm Veling. 2017. "Spontaneous Hedonic Reactions to Social Media Cues." *Cyberpsychology, Behavior, and Social Networking* 20(5): 334–340.

Vannini, Phillip (ed.). 2009. *Material Culture and Technology in Every Day: Ethnographic Approaches*. New York: Peter Lang.

Vannini, Phillip, Dennis Waskul, and Simon Gottschalk. 2011. *The Senses in Self, Society, and Culture: A Sociology of the Senses*. New York: Routledge.

Virilio, Paul, Friedrich Kittler, and John Armitage. 1999. "The Information Bomb: A Conversation." *Angelaki: Journal of the Theoretical Humanities*, 4(2): 81–90. http://dx.doi.org/10.1080/09697259908572036.

Wajcman, Judy. 2008. "Life in the Fast Lane? Towards a Sociology of Technology and Time." *The British Journal of Sociology* 59(1): 59–77.

Waldvogel, Joan. 2007. "Greetings and Closings in Workplace E-mail." *Journal of Computer-Mediated Communication* 12: 456–477.

Wallace, Patricia. 1999. *The Psychology of the Internet*. Cambridge University Press.

Weigert, Andrew J. 1997. *Self, Interaction and Natural Environment: Refocusing our Eyesight*. Albany: SUNY Press.

Wesselmann, Eric D. and Kipling D. Williams. 2011. "Being Ignored and Excluded in Electronic-Based Interactions." pp. 127–144 in *Strategic Uses of Social Technology: An Interactive Perspective of Social Psychology*, Zachary Birchmeier, Beth Dietz-Uhler, and Garold Stasser (eds.). Cambridge University Press.

Williams, Kipling D., Christopher K. T. Cheung, and Wilma Choi. 2000. "Cyberostracism: Effects of Being Ignored over the Internet." *Journal of Personality and Social Psychology* 79(5): 748–762.

Williams, Ray. 2014. "The Cult of Ignorance in the United States: Anti-Intellectualism and the 'Dumbing Down' of America." www.psychologytoday.com. Retrieved June 7, 2014.

Winkin, Yves. 1981. *La Nouvelle Communication*. Paris: éditions du Seuil.

Wittezele, Jean-Jacques and Teresa Garcia. 1992. *A La Recherche de L'école de Palo Alto*. Paris: éditions du Seuil.

Woodward, Ian. 2009. "Material Culture and Narrative: Fusing Myth, Materiality, and Meaning." pp. 59–72 in *Material Culture and Technology in Every Day: Ethnographic Approaches*, Phillip Vannini (ed.). New York: Peter Lang.

Zawadzki, Paul. 2011. "Le Regard Vertical." pp. 293–302 in *Les Tyrannies de la Visibilité: Être Visible Pour Exister?*, Nicole Aubert and Claudine Haroche (eds.). Toulouse: Erès.

Zerubavel, Eviatar. 1985. *Hidden Rhythms: Schedules and Calendars in Social Life*. Berkeley, CA: University of California Press.

Zerzan, John. 2006. "Youth and Regression in an Infantile Society." Retrieved March 30. www.primitivism.com.

Zimbardo, Phillip and Nikita D. Coulombe. 2015. *Man (Dis)connected: How Technology Has Sabotaged What It Means To Be Male*. London: Rider.

Zuboff, Shoshana. 2015. "Big Other: Surveillance Capitalism and the Prospects of an Information Civilization." *Journal of Information Technology* (30): 75–89.

Index